W9-APR-906

At Issue

Do Veterans Receive Adequate Health Care?

Other Books in the At Issue Series:

At Issue

Do Veterans Receive Adequate Health Care?

Susan Hunnicutt, Book Editor

GREENHAVEN PRESS
A part of Gale, Cengage Learning

GALE
CENGAGE Learning·

Detroit • New York • San Francisco • New Haven, Conn • Waterville, Maine • London

Elizabeth Des Chenes, *Director, Publishing Solutions*

© 2012 Greenhaven Press, a part of Gale, Cengage Learning.

Gale and Greenhaven Press are registered trademarks used herein under license.

For more information, contact:
Greenhaven Press
27500 Drake Rd.
Farmington Hills, MI 48331-3535
Or you can visit our Internet site at gale.cengage.com

For product information and technology assistance, contact us at

Gale Customer Support, 1-800-877-4253
For permission to use material from this text or product, submit all requests online at www.cengage.com/permissions.

Further permissions questions can be e-mailed to permissionrequest@cengage.com.

Articles in Greenhaven Press anthologies are often edited for length to meet page requirements. In addition, original titles of these works are changed to clearly present the main thesis and to explicitly indicate the author's opinion. Every effort is made to ensure that Greenhaven Press accurately reflects the original intent of the authors. Every effort has been made to trace the owners of copyrighted material.

Cover image copyright © Images.com/Corbis.

LIBRARY OF CONGRESS CATALOGING-IN-PUBLICATION DATA

Do veterans receive adequate health care? / Susan Hunnicutt, book editor.
    p. cm. -- (At issue)
Includes bibliographical references and index.
ISBN 978-0-7377-6169-6 (hbk.) -- ISBN 978-0-7377-6170-2 (pbk.)
1. Veterans--Medical care--United States. I. Hunnicutt, Susan.
UB369.D6 2012
362.1086'970973--dc23
                                                    2012007095

Printed in the United States of America
1 2 3 4 5 6 7 16 15 14 13 12

Contents

Introduction

In April 2011 employees of the Los Angeles Regional Office of the U.S. Department of Veterans Affairs (VA) reported that they were struggling under a backlog of more than 12,800 benefits claims, and that more than 3,100 claims appeals filed through their office were unresolved. According to the County of San Bernardino Department of Veterans Affairs—a local agency that assists veterans in applying for benefits—individuals served by the VA's regional office in Los Angeles could expect to wait 12 to 18 months for an initial claim to be completed. It was common for appeals to remain unresolved for several years. A message on the organization's website counseled quiet patience: "In order to reduce unnecessary demands on the VA staff processing your claim, our Director . . . has instructed our staff not to check on claims until at least six months have passed from the date the claim was filed. Frequent checking on the status of a claim prevents the VA from doing their job."

Conditions in the Los Angeles Regional Office mirrored the situation in VA offices nation-wide: The total number of pending actions for veterans' benefits at the time was 512,000 claims and 90,800 appeals.

The following month, the U.S. Court of Appeals for the 9th Circuit ruled in a 104-page opinion that delays in medical care resulting from the VA's claims backlogs deprived veterans of their constitutional rights. The 2-1 decision, in a case originally filed by two veterans' organizations (Veterans for Common Sense and Veterans United for Truth) in the Northern District of California on July 23, 2007, was subsequently withdrawn after an appeal from the VA. The court is expected to issue a new ruling in the future, although the date for a hearing has not been scheduled.

While the May 2011 ruling is no longer in force, it does indicate the opposing opinions of members of the three-judge panel at the time it was made.

"Veterans who return home from war suffering from psychological maladies are entitled by law to disability benefits to sustain themselves and their families as they regain their health," Judge Stephen Reinhardt wrote, for the court's majority. "Yet it takes an average of more than four years for a veteran to fully adjudicate a claim for benefits. During that time many claims are mooted by deaths. . . . For veterans and their families, such delays cause unnecessary grief and privation. And for some veterans, most notably those suffering from combat-derived mental illnesses such as PTSD [post-traumatic stress disorder], these delays may make the difference between life and death."

Judge Alex Kozinski, the dissenting judge, argued that the court was constitutionally limited in its ability to resolve the matter in the veterans' favor. "Much as the VA's failure to meet the needs of veterans with PTSD might shock and outrage us, we may not step in and boss it around," he said. Kozinski, who urged mediation, argued that it was the job of the executive and legislative branches of the government, and not the courts, to assure adequate provision for benefits claims filed by veterans.

The VA has also argued that the courts are not authorized to adjudicate claims for veterans' benefits.

The backdrop of the Appeals Court's action was, and continues to be, grim. Veterans groups claim that between 100,000 and 300,000 service members are suffering from PTSD, a mental health condition that can develop in the aftermath of terrifying events. Events leading to the development of full-blown PTSD can include working in combat zones where constant vigilance is required for extended periods of time, training accidents, military sexual assault, and being a witness to a medical emergency. Symptoms of PTSD include flashbacks, nightmares, persistent anxiety and the inability to control thoughts and memories related to the triggering events.

Abundant evidence supports the claim that hundreds of thousands of veterans are suffering from PTSD, and that the personal and social costs are enormous. The Veterans Health Administration has itself reported a 34 percent increase in the number of veterans using VA mental health services between FY [fiscal year] 2006 and FY 2010. Almost forty percent of mental health professionals employed in the VA say they are not able to schedule appointments within the 14 days that the agency itself says are required. Seventy percent say that resources, including both staff and facilities, are inadequate to meet the mental health care needs of the veterans they serve. The House Committee on Veterans Affairs estimates that 950 veterans being treated by the VA attempt suicide every month, and information released by the Department of Defense shows that a service member committed suicide every 36 hours from 2005 to 2010.

In addition to the epidemic of suicides among both enlisted soldiers and veterans, it is widely believed that the inability to access treatment for PTSD has and will continue to result in broken relationships, family violence, and the loss of jobs and homes.

Do veterans of the wars in Iraq and Afghanistan have a constitutional right to the timely and efficient handling of their treatment and benefits claims? This is one of many urgent and unresolved questions that emerges from the viewpoints that are represented in *At Issue: Do Veterans Receive Adequate Health Care?*

1

Military and Veterans' Health Care: An Overview

The Kaiser Family Foundation

The Kaiser Family Foundation is a non-profit institution that focuses attention on major health care issues facing the US, as well as the US role in global health policy.

Several agencies exist to serve the health care needs of active and retired members of the US armed services. These include Tricare for active duty military, the Veterans Health Administration for veterans, and CHAMPVA for eligible spouses and dependent children of disabled and deceased veterans. Veterans are also entitled to disability compensation for medical conditions, including mental health conditions, associated with their military service.

Overview

Military health care encompasses a diverse range of programs, each serving a total military population of more than 9.2 million people, including active duty personnel and families, retirees and their families, and eligible veterans. The major military health care programs are operated through the Department of Defense (DoD) and the Department of Veterans Affairs. The Department of Defense covers active duty service members and retirees from all branches of the military and their families while the Department of Veterans Affairs covers veterans and their eligible family members.[1] Each program has different eligibility criteria, benefits packages, and financing structures.

Active Duty and Military Personnel

The Department of Defense purchases and provides health care for approximately 8.3 million beneficiaries, including active duty personnel and retirees, and their family members. The Department's health care is provided at more than 530 Army, Navy, and Air Force military treatment facilities worldwide and is supplemented by the TRICARE program's network of civilian providers through contracts with civilian managed health care providers. TRICARE covers active duty service members, retirees, activated Guards/Reserves, and their family members, providing them with government-subsidized medical and dental care. The Army, Navy, and Air Force each have a surgeon general who directs the military providers in each branch and acts as a health care advisor to the Secretary of the respective branch.

TRICARE

TRICARE is the Department of Defense's managed health care program for active duty military, active duty service families, retirees and their families, and other beneficiaries from any of the seven services—Army, Navy, Marine Corps, Air Force, Coast Guard, Public Health Service, and National Oceanic and Atmospheric Administration as well as select National Reserve and Guard members. National Reservists and Guards on active duty for more than 30 consecutive days have comprehensive health care coverage under TRICARE. Their family members' health and dental care are also covered under several TRICARE program options.

Beneficiaries can choose from three health coverage plans: (1) TRICARE Prime, the HMO option of TRICARE; (2) TRICARE Extra, which has a larger provider network but also a deductible; (3) TRICARE Standard, formerly known as

11

CHAMPUS. While the benefits are the same across all three plans, there are differences in who is eligible, the provider networks, and the out-of-pocket costs under each plan.[2] In addition, the TRICARE Reserve Select program is a health plan that eligible National Guard and Reserve members can buy into by paying monthly premiums, and the program is open to most members of the Reserves who are not on active duty. Covered benefits are comparable to TRICARE Extra and Standard packages.

> *The VHA operates the nation's largest integrated health care system, and provides care to over 5 million inpatients and outpatients.*

TRICARE for Life (TFL) is available to Medicare-eligible military retirees and their family members and survivors who are enrolled in Medicare Part B. For services covered by both Medicare and TRICARE, Medicare acts as the first payer and TRICARE pays the remaining out-of-pocket costs. Unlike the other TRICARE programs, TRICARE for LIFE is an entitlement program so it does not require annual renewals by Congress.

Veterans

Veterans Affairs

The Veterans Health Administration (VHA) is the branch of the U.S. Department of Veterans Affairs that purchases coverage for and delivers health care to veterans and their families. The VHA operates the nation's largest integrated health care system, and provides care to over 5 million inpatients and outpatients at its vast network of hospitals, outpatient clinics, nursing homes, residential rehabilitation treatment programs, and readjustment counseling centers.[3]

Eligibility for VA health care benefits depends solely on active military service in the Army, Navy, Air Force, Marines, or

Coast Guard. Most of the nation's 24 million veterans are eligible for some aspect of VA's health care services if they choose to enroll. Enrolled veterans are assigned to one of eight priority levels (P1 through P8) based on their service-connected disabilities, income levels, and other factors. Under this priority system, the Secretary of Veterans Affairs decides each year whether VA's medical budget is adequate to serve veterans in all priority groups who seek care.

Historically a health care system serving only veterans with service-connected disabilities, the VA is now open to all veterans and has become an important "safety net" for many low-income veterans who would otherwise be uninsured. However, 1.8 million U.S. veterans under age 65 continue to lack health insurance or access to care at Veterans Affairs hospitals as of 2004. This means that one in eight, or 12.7 percent of non-elderly veterans are uninsured, up from 9.9 percent in 2000.[4] About half of the 1.8 million uninsured veterans are classified in the lowest priority group (P8), and are not currently eligible for VA healthcare, while the rest may be eligible, but live too far from VA facilities to access services.[5]

The VA provides a uniform Medical Benefits Package to all enrolled veterans, covering preventive and primary care, outpatient and inpatient services within the VA health care system, and prescription drugs. Based on priority status, the VA provides additional services, such as nursing home and dental care, for some veterans and makes these services available to other veterans on a discretionary basis as resources permit.

There are over 9.5 million U.S. veterans who are over 65 years of age and eligible for both VA health care and Medicare. Currently, veterans who are enrolled in both Medicare and VA health must choose either Medicare or VA to pay for services each time they need care. And while Medicare-eligible veterans are unable to use Medicare coverage at VA hospitals and facilities, Medicare can help pay for some co-payments charged by the VA.

CHAMPVA

CHAMPVA (Civilian Health and Medical Program of the Department of Veteran Affairs) provides medical care for spouses and dependent children of disabled or deceased disabled veterans who meet the eligibility requirements of the Veterans Administration. Qualified beneficiaries of CHAMPVA receive coverage for the same package of benefits offered under traditional VA, and seek care within the VA network of providers.

Financing

Services received by active duty military personnel and their families are funded through Congressional appropriations to the Department of Defense budget, as is TRICARE. The Department of Defense uses the Medicare Eligible Retiree Health Care Fund (MERHCF) to pay for health benefits for Medicare eligible Department of Defense military retirees, retiree family members, and survivors up to age 65.

> *One issue that challenges both the VA and Department of Defense is the transition process for service members moving from active duty into the VA health care system.*

Congress also appropriates funds annually for the VA to provide health care services to eligible veterans. Since demand is often greater than available resources, veterans assigned to higher priorities are enrolled first with the possibility that those in lower priorities may not receive care. While funding levels for the VA have increased in each of the President's budget requests for fiscal years 2003 through 2006, the proposals assumed that management efficiency initiatives that would save money without compromising access or quality. However, these savings have failed to materialize, resulting in a funding shortfall.[6]

Coordination

One issue that challenges both the VA and Department of Defense is the transition process for service members moving from active duty into the VA health care system. The VA and Department of Defense operate distinct systems that offer differing levels of benefits and often use different standards for assessing severity of illness or injuries. These differences have resulted in some gaps in medical service.[7]

Quality

The Department of Veterans Affairs has been recognized as a leader in improving the quality of health care, including pioneering work in the implementation of technologies and systems to improve the delivery of care.[8] VA leadership has also been recognized for the establishment of a quality measurement program that holds regional managers accountable for processes in preventive care and in the management of common chronic conditions. The Department of Defense also has undertaken major quality improvement initiatives. However, there have been some difficulties in sharing information between the two departments in part because the two Departments have differing interpretations of federal privacy provisions governing the sharing of individually identifiable health data.[9] The difficulties experienced by disabled soldiers and the coordination of their care as they transition to civilian life has been a major driver of recent legislative efforts, congressional hearings and federal investigations to improve support services for veterans returning from Iraq and Afghanistan.[10]

Disability

Compensation

The U.S. government has long recognized the need to provide disability compensation to veterans for health problems associated with military service. Veterans must undergo medical evaluations for each condition they are claiming and must file claims with the Veterans Benefits Administration, which rate service-related injuries on a sliding scale. These ratings assess the effects on earning capacity from such injuries and disabilities. However, the fairness of this approach has raised concern because while a disability may not impair the ability to work in many occupations, it may still significantly affect quality of life, which has historically not been a major factor in disability ratings.[11]

Mental Health

One common type of health problem for which disability compensation is requested is mental health conditions. Exposure to a combat environment can disrupt civilian life and can have a strong impact on a service member's mental health and psychological well-being. Among just the U.S. troops returning from Iraq and Afghanistan, nearly 40 percent of soldiers, a third of Marines, and half of the National Guard members report symptoms of psychological problems. Of note has been the increasing incidence of post-traumatic stress disorder (PTSD), a psychiatric disorder that can occur following the experience or witnessing of life-threatening events such as military combat, natural disasters, or violent personal assaults like rape. Another overarching concern is the stigma associated with disclosing mental health symptoms and asking for help within the military culture, both within the armed services and to a lesser extent in VA settings. The Department of Defense has been working on mental health services, particularly improving post-deployment mental health assessments to better understand the psychological effects of combat and related mental health care needs of those returning from combat.[12]

Conclusion

Given the growing need for providing health care and related benefits to the nation's service members, policymakers will continue to focus on strengthening both the Department of

Defense Military Health System and the Department of VA health care system, which operate in parallel and in conjunction with each other. There is also greater emphasis in policy circles on ensuring a "seamless transition" process for service members moving from active duty into the VA health care system. Areas of focused attention include coordination between health and other benefits offered by the DoD and the VA, improving care for injured service members, and easing the transition from combat service to other military or civilian life.

Notes

1. U.S. Government Accountability Office, VA and DoD Health Care: Opportunities to Maximize Resource Sharing Remain, March 2006.
2. U.S. Department of Defense Military Health System.
3. Congressional Budget Office, The Health Care System for Veterans, December 2007.
4. Woolhandler, S., Uninsured Veterans: A Stain on American's Flag, Testimony to the House Committee on Veterans Affairs on June 20, 2007.
5. Department of Veteran Affairs, Enrollment Priority Groups, March 2007.
6. U.S. Government Accountability Office, Veterans Affairs: Limited Support for Reported Health Care Management Efficiency Savings, February 1, 2006.
7. Bascetta, C.A., U.S. Government Accountability Office, DoD and VA Health Care: Challenges Encountered by Injured Service Members During Their Recovery, Testimony to the House Subcommittee on Oversight and Investigations on March 8, 2007.
8. Glaser, J. Testimony to U.S. Senate Committee on Veterans Affairs, September 19, 2007.
9. U.S. Government Accountability Office, VA and DoD Efforts to Exchange Health Data Could Benefit from Improved Planning and Project Management, July 7, 2004.

10. Meeting the Health Care Needs of Returning Service Members and New Veterans, Hearing of the U.S. Senate Veterans Affairs Committee, March 27, 2007; Hearing on Mental Health Problems Confronting Soldiers Returning from Iraq, Afghanistan, U.S. House of Representatives Oversight and Government Reform Committee, May 24, 2007.

11. Committee on Medical Evaluation of Veterans in Disability Compensation, Institute of Medicine, A 21st Century System for Evaluating Veterans for Disability Benefits, 2007.

12. Department of Defense Task Force on Mental Health, An Achievable Vision: Report of the Department of Defense Task Force on Mental Health, June 2007.

2

Veterans Administration Health Care Is Among the Best in the U.S.

Kristen Gerencher

Kristen Gerencher is a reporter and columnist for MarketWatch, *a publication of* The Wall Street Journal.

The Veterans Health Administration, which is financed with tax-payer dollars, has adopted a number of quality improvement measures such as information systems and support tools, coordinated care, and long-term relationships between patients and health care providers that have made it a leader in health care quality. The administration continues to adapt and focus on areas of improvement, such as services for women veterans.

W*here can you find the highest quality health care in the U.S.? There isn't one single answer, but believe it or not, many studies and independent experts point to the Veterans Health Administration [VA] as among the best.*

The VA has its own system-wide electronic health record, sophisticated quality-measurement tools, a coordinated approach to care, long relationships with patients and close ties to teaching hospitals, which supply a steady stream of medical residents.

Some other health systems also provide excellent patient care, and every place has it weaknesses, but the VA generally stands out on quality, said Elizabeth McGlynn, associate director of Rand Health, a division of the Rand Corp., in Santa Monica, [California].

"You're much better off in the VA than in a lot of the rest of the U.S. health-care system," she said. "You've got a fighting chance there's going to be some organized, thoughtful, evidence-based response to dealing effectively with the health problem that somebody brings to them."

The VA outperformed its community health-care counterparts by 20 percentage points in preventive care. It also performed significantly better on chronic disease care and in overall quality.

The combination of its information system and support tools, routine performance reporting and financial incentives for managers who hit quality targets gives it an edge, said McGlynn, who co-authored a comparative study published in the *Annals of Internal Medicine* in 2004 that found the VA outperformed its community health-care counterparts by 20 percentage points in preventive care. It also performed significantly better on chronic disease care and in overall quality.

As the U.S. enters a new era with the passage of the health-reform law that takes full effect in 2014, experts say the VA's evolution offers lessons because many of the pilot projects and quality-improvement initiatives the new law calls for are similar to the VA's approach.

Why It's Different

The VA expects to treat 5.5 million veterans in the U.S., Puerto Rico, U.S. Virgin Islands and Guam this year [2010] the majority of whom have medical problems related to their military service. Financed by taxpayer dollars, it has a current health-care budget of $50 billion and operates more than 1,400 care sites, including 950 outpatient clinics, 153 hospitals and 134 nursing homes.

Health-care providers practice in teams and doctors are salaried as opposed to being paid a fee for service. That helps remove an incentive to order tests and procedures that aren't necessary, a key problem in the broader U.S. health system when physicians practice defensive medicine or try to maximize their income, said Phillip Longman, senior fellow at the New America Foundation and author of a book about the VA called "Best Care Anywhere."

"The rest of the health-care system doesn't have a business case for quality," Longman said. "Quality usually costs them money because they get paid to perform procedures on sick people."

"There are many idealistic people in medicine trying to do the right thing, but in our system no good deed goes unpunished," he said, citing diabetes care as an example.

"The big money is in letting diabetics decline to the point they need an amputation, need dialysis, become blind. That's where you make your big money, not in keeping them well. Once you know a little about how this world works, it stands to reason the VA's the best care," Longman said.

Dr. Ashish Jha, associate professor of health policy at Harvard School of Public Health and a general internist at the Boston VA, won't go as far as to say the VA is superior to other medical stand-outs in the broader health-care system.

"What I do know is that the care in the VA is consistently very good and certainly much better than average," Jha said.

It has imposed market-based reforms such as pay for performance and value-based purchasing that have paid off, he said.

"They have in some ways brought the rules of supply and demand to bear in assuring the care they deliver is much more efficient," Jha said. "I do think there's something ironic about that, that a government agency was doing it before the private sector was."

The VA isn't a likely candidate for achieving such gains given that it's run by a sprawling federal agency, has five public-sector labor unions and a patient population that tends to be older, sicker and poorer than average, Longman said. But its success is more commonly accepted now than even a few years ago.

The rest of the health-care system is about 15 years behind not just in health-information-technology implementation but also in moving toward a patient-centered care model.

"You're seeing a lot of people who may have served in Vietnam and had very bad images of the VA," Longman said. "They never went to it or they went to it once and had a bad experience and are now coming back in their 50s, 60s, and 70s [saying] 'This place is great. The drugs are cheap. There's a whole team looking at me. Their computers remind me every year I'm due for a flu shot and it's kind of one-stop shopping.'"

Longman estimates the rest of the health-care system is about 15 years behind not just in health-information-technology implementation but also in moving toward a patient-centered care model.

To be sure, the VA has had its share of scandals and lapses over the years. Last year, two VA centers in Florida and Tennessee contacted thousands of veterans to alert them that they may have been exposed to contaminated colonoscopy equipment that could put them at risk for hepatitis or HIV.

But despite such sporadic problems, many experts credit the VA with staging a remarkable turnaround in the mid-1990s that now puts it among the highest-performing systems on many measures of quality ranging from the effective treatment of diabetes to the reduction of medication-dispensing errors.

Meeting New Challenges

A key challenge is how the VA will continue to adapt as health care increasingly moves away from hospital-based settings and becomes more outpatient-oriented.

And even with its electronic health record called VistA, it too will have to hustle to meet younger veterans' expectations for customer service and technological capacity, Jha said.

"These are folks who grew up in the Facebook generation, and they expect a level of use of technology and responsiveness that's going to be tough for any agency to meet," he said.

Among the most pressing concerns is how the VA can keep pace with the needs of women veterans, a growing subgroup of its patients.

At many VA facilities, women still can't receive comprehensive primary care at one site, according to a March report from the Government Accountability Office, an independent body that advises Congress. The report found the VA is having trouble recruiting mental-health care providers who can treat military sexual trauma specific to women, and needs to better address the privacy and safety needs of female veterans.

Denise Williams, 33, is familiar with the VA's strengths and shortcomings. Having served in the army in a noncombat role for seven years until 2003, she now goes to the VA Medical Center in Washington three or four times a year for routine health care and once a year for well-woman checkups.

"There's still staff members that need to be trained to realize women are veterans," she said. "Sometimes a female veteran is mistaken for the spouse."

Overall, Williams said she's satisfied with the VA care she receives. "There are still gaps that need to be filled and they still have a way to go, but I think it's a very good health-care system."

As is customary, she was assigned a primary-care doctor as part of her health-care team and is happy enough with that relationship that she hasn't requested a physician switch. She also likes how flexible the pharmacy options are.

"You can call for your refills and they'll mail it in," Williams said. "They're very reliable. If you don't have the time to wait and pick it up yourself, you can request it gets mailed to your home."

She said paperless health records make for more seamless care than when she was in the military, and she currently pays no copays. But if she's seeking care for a health problem that's not service-connected, it can take a few weeks to be seen.

3

The Veterans Administration Provides Inadequate Care in Many Cases

Melissa Suran

Melissa Suran wrote this article while she was a graduate student in journalism at the Medill School at Northwestern University.

Veterans suffering from post-traumatic stress disorder (PTSD) and other illnesses as a result of their combat experience often encounter difficulty getting treatment. Many veterans blame inadequate funding and inadequate staffing at Department of Veterans Affairs hospitals.

The heavy smell of Asian food was in the air. Street vendors were selling fresh groceries, parents were buying their children cheap good-luck charms, and the chatter of everyone could be heard throughout the square. It was like any other day for Sgt. Gil Rivera, who vividly recalls the midday scene.

Suddenly, Rivera heard some voices speaking in Vietnamese. A soldier in the Vietnam War, he was ready to kill the passersby, whose voices were coming closer and closer.

But he didn't have his gun. And he wasn't in Vietnam. In fact, he was in New York—in Chinatown.

The incident occurred about 30 years after the Vietnam War. Rivera, who served in the U.S. Army, said what happened to him was a reaction caused by Post Traumatic Stress Disorder, or PTSD, a mental illness that can result from being in a terrifying situation where one's physical well-being is threatened.

Obama said he plans to do much more financially for veterans who suffer from mental illnesses resulting from war.

PTSD Is Not the Same as Post Traumatic Stress

Post Traumatic Stress Disorder is not to be confused with Post Traumatic Stress, or PTS, which results directly from a traumatic event or from trauma. Although many who suffer from PTS personally underwent a terrible experience, PTS can also be caused by witnessing a traumatic event. Patients are diagnosed with Post Traumatic Stress Disorder when PTS symptoms last for a month or more.

Although many experience PTS, it does not always rise to the level of a being a disorder. Symptoms of PTS include being angered easily or having unpleasant emotions triggered by sensory perception such as sound or smell.

It took Rivera three decades to get the help he needed and he is now fully pensioned. Unfortunately, his case is an all-too-common one.

"I hadn't heard Vietnamese spoken since Vietnam," said Rivera, 63, who now lives in Prince Frederick, Md. "Honestly, if I had a gun who knows, maybe I would have shot those people."

Rivera is one of more than 1 million veterans who suffer from PTSD. But Rivera is lucky that he received any help at all.

On Aug. 17 [2009] at the Veterans of Foreign Wars National Convention in Phoenix, President Barack Obama said he plans to do more when it comes to veterans' health care.

The President Has Promised Change

"We are a country of more than 300 million Americans. Less than one percent wears the uniform," he said. "As we protect America, our men and women in uniform must always be treated as what they are: America's most precious resource."

Obama said he plans to do much more financially for veterans who suffer from mental illnesses resulting from war.

"Every dollar wasted in our defense budget is a dollar we can't spend to care for our troops," Obama said. "For so many veterans the war rages on—the flashbacks that won't go away, the loved ones who now seem like strangers, the heavy darkness of depression that has led too many of our troops to take their own lives. Post Traumatic Stress and Traumatic Brain Injury are the defining injuries of today's wars. So, caring for those affected by them is a defining purpose of my budget . . . we will not abandon these American heroes."

In his speech, Obama promised to pour billions of dollars into veterans' health care while "restoring access to VA health care for a half-million veterans who lost their eligibility in recent years."

There are over 1 million American veterans without health insurance.

The Long Road to Diagnosis

Back when Rivera first noticed signs of his PTSD during the war, the disorder wasn't even recognized as an illness.

"It took me about 30 years to find out I had PTSD," Rivera said. "In those 30 years I tried to control my own nightmares, I worked long hours and slept very little, I got in into fist fights, arguments, I drank like a fish . . . once I found out what it was because I studied it, I was able to take control of it."

Nevertheless, Rivera continued to resent the Department of Veterans Affairs [VA] for disregarding his illness.

"We got no help from the VA, from anyone," he said.

And many veterans still don't today.

According to a report issued by Harvard University in 2007, there are over 1 million American veterans without health insurance and 3.8 million members of veteran households who are also without health insurance—and the number continues to grow.

Rivera said the VA forces veterans to bend over backwards to prove they have current problems caused by a war that took place decades ago.

"What I've seen . . . at the VA is that they give you a lot of lip service about how they treat the vets," said Rivera, who also helps counsel veterans finding difficulty getting benefits. "When you see them on TV saying how much we want to help you, blah, blah, blah, that's all bull."

The VA Creates Obstacles to Care

According to Rivera, the reason is that the VA does not want to provide so many people with benefits.

"They give you a hard time and make it as hard as possible," he said.

For example, Rivera said many veterans who have skin issues, kidney problems, prostate cancer or even diabetes believe their health issues resulted from exposure to Agent Orange. Because they cannot prove the symptoms are directly linked to the herbicide exposure, the VA denies the veterans coverage.

However, representatives from the Department of Veterans Affairs hospitals say that it isn't so. In fact, they claim to encourage veterans to seek proper care at designated hospitals.

"When military personnel receive deployment to Iraq and Afghanistan, once they completed that deployment, they are guaranteed five years of care from the time of their deployment," said Kate Chard, the director of the PTSD Division at Cincinnati VA Medical Center.

If the five-year window has passed, Chard said veterans may file claims in a veterans service office. After a veteran files a claim, a therapist reviews it. The veterans may also bring supporting documents, deployment records, employment records, documents of medication problems and anything else to strengthen their case. They may also provide evidence of where they were stationed during their service and whether there was combat in the area, which could lead to PTSD.

Brian Morris, 36, a litigation attorney at the John Marshall Law School in Chicago, said he constantly deals with veterans who are not getting sufficient care—or any care, for that matter.

Most VA medical centers do not have enough high-quality doctors on staff.

Lack of Doctors Is a Problem

"Getting affordable ... medical and therapeutic care is probably [veterans'] biggest hurdle," Morris said. "As an institution, the VA certainly tries to assist everyone they can, but their budget constraints and personnel constraints often times result in a standard of care that is unacceptable."

Morris, who was diagnosed with PTSD from a tour in Iraq as an Army Reserve major, said the problem is primarily a resource issue, as most VA medical centers do not have enough high-quality doctors on staff.

Additionally, veterans with emotional effects of war depend on the VA for the costs that private insurance companies won't cover. Without the VA, many veterans cannot afford mental-health expenses. According to Morris, many times the VA will label a veteran's disorder as a preexisting condition, not caused by warfare.

As a result, Morris said many veterans find themselves with three options.

"They can go back to the VA and accept the level of care from them, whatever that is, or go to the outside world, use private insurance and pay the difference, or they don't get any care at all," he said.

Morris, who was a legal assistant in Baghdad in 2005 and counseled soldiers under Gen. David Petraeus, is no stranger to PTSD. He plans to deploy to Afghanistan in the next couple of months.

PTSD Can Make a Person Prefer Combat

Morris said because of his PTSD, he actually prefers to be in a combat zone rather than go through the anxieties and pressures of "ordinary" life.

"You feel normal [on the battlefield], you don't feel like an oddball . . . you don't have the need to explain anything," he said. "The military takes most of the decision making in your life away from you, so in some ways it's much easier than living in the real world where you get up every day and go to work."

And that's another thing, Morris said—not many people take the time to understand what it's like to suffer from PTSD.

Chard, the VA official, said as soon as a veteran believes he has a problem, he should immediately look into whether or not he is eligible for care.

"There's always an office they can go to," Chard said.

According to the VA, the only ways to not qualify for care would be if a veteran received a dishonorable discharge or had injuries or illnesses that are not in any way related to his or her military service.

"I have many stories where patients came back from Vietnam and then they immerse themselves in work, got divorced or retire, and realize, 'Oh gosh, I never went to the VA, I never had myself established, what am I going to do?' And then they establish a claim and lo-and-behold, they are found to have full-blown PTSD and they have coverage," Chard said.

According to Chard, 70 percent of those treated properly for PTSD get better, another reason she said it's very important to get treated.

"You need to get in that window of eligibility," she said. "Just because you didn't go [get help from the VA] when you came home, that doesn't mean there's no hope for you . . . it doesn't mean you're not eligible."

When someone does not qualify for care, Chard refers the patient to a Vet Center.

"The centers are a lot smaller . . . they have peer support groups where you can get that connection . . . [it's] a nice augment . . . for patients not eligible for VA care," she said.

Morris disagrees—especially when it comes to treating veterans who just served in Iraq.

Veterans Centers Are Not a Solution for Younger Vets

"The problem with Vet Centers is that they're pretty much filled with Vietnam vets," he said. "A lot of Vietnam vets are drug and alcohol dependent, homeless and the Vet Centers are filled with these individuals." . . .

"People who are younger don't want to be surrounded by grandpa," Morris said. "They think, 'Grandpa is drinking alcohol because he served in 1968 and he needs to move on. I better not be fighting a war that grandpa fought—I don't want to listen to him all day.'"

However, Rivera, who also counsels veterans suffering from PTSD, thinks that just having someone to listen to you can make all the difference.

Although now fully pensioned under the VA, Rivera still volunteers his time to helping his fellow veterans because he feels his country lacks in that area.

Although there is much work to be done, Rivera said he's impressed with Obama's attempt to fix this problem.

"This new administration is putting a lot of money into VA services, so things are slowly beginning to change," he said.

Rivera hopes more drastic changes will happen sooner rather than later—especially for the soldiers who suffer from mental anguish as he does.

"I can't control the feeling—it's like a hallucination," Rivera said. "It's like I'm actually there at that moment . . . I feel the heat, I smell the smells, I'm in combat and in that moment it's real. But in the back of my head I know it's not."

4

America Must Fulfill Its Obligations to Its Wounded Veterans

Barack Obama

President Barack Obama delivered this speech, "Remarks by the President on Improving Veterans' Health Care," in Washington, DC on April 9, 2009.

America's servicemen and women have demonstrated honor, sacrifice and commitment, and many of them have suffered injuries or debilitating illnesses as a result. Too often, they have not received adequate support to start new lives once their service is completed. The US will provide the stable stream of funding that is needed to support state-of-the-art veterans' health care, as well as to provide opportunities for veterans to own a home and attend college.

To the VSO [Veterans Service Organization] and MSO [Military Service Organization] leaders who work hard on behalf of those who serve this nation, thank you for your advocacy and your hard work. As I look out in the audience, especially seeing these folks in their uniforms, I am reminded of the fact that we have the best fighting force in world history, and the reason we do is because of all of you. And so I'm very grateful for what you've done to protect and serve this country.

It is good to be back. We've had a productive week working to advance America's interests around the world. We

President Barack Obama, "Remarks by the President on Improving Veterans' Health Care," The White House, April 9, 2009. www.whitehouse.gov.

worked to renew our alliances to enhance our common security. We collaborated with other nations to take steps towards rebuilding the global economy, which will revitalize our own.

A Grateful Nation Says "Thank You"

And before coming home, I stopped to visit with our men and women who are serving bravely in Iraq. First and foremost, I wanted to say "thank you" to them on behalf of a grateful nation. They've faced extraordinary challenges, and they have performed brilliantly in every mission that's been given to them. They have given Iraq the opportunity to stand on its own as a democratic country, and that is a great gift.

You know, we often talk about ideals like sacrifice and honor and duty. But these men and women, like the men and women who are here, embody it. They have made sacrifices many of us cannot begin to imagine.

We're talking about men like Specialist Jake Altman and Sergeant Nathan Dewitt, two of the soldiers who I had the honor to meet when I was in Baghdad. In 2007, as Specialist Altman was clearing mines so that other soldiers might travel in safety, he lost his hand when an IED [improvised explosive device] struck his vehicle. And at Walter Reed, he asked to re-learn the skills necessary to perform his duties with a prosthetic so that he could rejoin his old battalion. Sergeant Dewitt was severely injured in an attack last September, but he refused to let his injuries stop him from giving first aid to his wounded comrades. Today, they're both back alongside their fellow soldiers in their old units.

They Are Heroes

And we're talking about women like Tammy Duckworth, who I think is here—Tammy, where are you? There you are—a great friend who lost her legs when a rocket struck the Black Hawk helicopter she was piloting over Iraq. And when she returned home, she continued to serve her country heading the

Department of Veterans Affairs in Illinois, and she serves her country still as my nominee for Assistant Secretary of the Department of Veterans Affairs.

We're talking about heroes like all the service members and veterans of the United States Armed Forces, including the veterans who've joined us here today—many who gave up much yet signed up to give more; many with their own battles still to come; all with their own stories to tell.

Too many wounded warriors go without the care that they need. . . . Too many who once wore our nation's uniform now sleep in our nation's streets.

For their service and sacrifice, warm words of thanks from a grateful nation are more than warranted, but they aren't nearly enough. We also owe our veterans the care they were promised and the benefits that they have earned. We have a sacred trust with those who wear the uniform of the United States of America. It's a commitment that begins at enlistment, and it must never end.

We Have a Debt to Pay

But we know that for too long, we've fallen short of meeting that commitment. Too many wounded warriors go without the care that they need. Too many veterans don't receive the support that they've earned. Too many who once wore our nation's uniform now sleep in our nation's streets.

It's time to change all that. It's time to give our veterans a 21st-century VA. Over the past few months we've made much progress towards that end, and today I'm pleased to announce some new progress.

Under the leadership of Secretary Gates and Secretary Shinseki, the Department of Defense and the Department of Veterans Affairs have taken a first step towards creating one unified lifetime electronic health record for members of our armed services that will contain their administrative and medical information—from the day they first enlist to the day that they are laid to rest.

Currently, there is no comprehensive system in place that allows for a streamlined transition of health records between DOD and the VA. And that results in extraordinary hardship for a awful lot of veterans, who end up finding their records lost, unable to get their benefits processed in a timely fashion. I can't tell you how many stories that I heard during the course of the last several years, first as a United States senator and then as a candidate, about veterans who were finding it almost impossible to get the benefits that they had earned despite the fact that their disabilities or their needs were evident for all to see.

And that's why I'm asking both departments to work together to define and build a seamless system of integration with a simple goal: When a member of the Armed Forces separates from the military, he or she will no longer have to walk paperwork from a DOD duty station to a local VA health center; their electronic records will transition along with them and remain with them forever.

Now, this would represent a huge step towards modernizing the way health care is delivered and benefits are administered for our nation's veterans. It would cut through red tape and reduce the number of administrative mistakes. It would allow all VA sites access to a veteran's complete military medical record, giving them the information they need to deliver high-quality care. And it would do all this with the strictest and most rigorous standards of privacy and security, so that our veterans can have confidence that their medical records can only be shared at their direction.

We Need to Stabilize Funding for Veterans' Health Care

Now, the care that our veterans receive should never be hindered by budget delays. I've shared this concern with Secretary

Shinseki, and we have worked together to support advanced funding for veterans' medical care. What that means is a timely and predictable flow of funding from year to year, but more importantly, that means better care for our veterans. And I was pleased to see that the budget resolution passed by the Senate supports this concept in a bipartisan manner.

This budget . . . significantly expands coverage so that 500,000 more veterans who have previously been denied it will receive it, and it strengthens care and services across a broad range of areas.

I'm also pleased that the budget resolutions adopted by both houses of Congress preserve priorities that I outlined in my budget—priorities that will go a long way towards building that 21st-century VA that we're looking for. The 2010 budget includes the largest single-year increase in VA funding in three decades. And all told, we will increase funding by $25 billion over the next five years.

This budget doesn't just signify increased funding for the VA health care program; it significantly expands coverage so that 500,000 more veterans who have previously been denied it will receive it, and it strengthens care and services across a broad range of areas.

The Deadliest Wounds Cannot Be Seen

Because the nightmares of war don't always end when our loved ones return home, this budget also meets the mental health needs of our wounded warriors. Untold thousands of servicemen and women returning from Iraq and Afghanistan suffer from Post-Traumatic Stress Disorder or other serious psychological injury. The growing incidence of suicide among active military returning veterans is disturbing. Sometimes the deadliest wounds are the ones you cannot see, and we cannot afford to let the unseen wounds go untreated. And that's why this budget dramatically increases funding for mental health screening and treatment at all levels. It increases the number of vet centers and mobile health clinics, expanding access to this needed care in rural areas. And it helps reduce the stigma of seeking care by adding mental health professionals to educate veterans and their families about their injuries and their options.

And because thousands of Iraq and Afghanistan veterans have suffered from Traumatic Brain Injury, one of the signature injuries of these wars, this budget improves services for cognitive injuries. And many with TBI have never been evaluated by a physician. And because such injuries can often have long-term impacts that only show up down the road, this funding will help ensure they receive the ongoing care they need.

It's our turn to help guarantee this generation the same opportunity that the greatest generation enjoyed by providing every returning service member with a real chance to afford a college education.

Because we all share the shame of 154,000 veterans going homeless on any given night, this budget also funds a pilot program with not-for-profit organizations to make sure that veterans at risk of losing their homes have a roof over their heads. And we will not rest until we reach a day when not one single veteran falls into homelessness.

This Is a Budget That Supports Dreams

Finally, this budget recognizes that our veterans deserve something more—an equal chance to reach for the very dream they defend. It's the chance America gave to my grandfather, who enlisted after Pearl Harbor and went on to march in Patton's Army. When he came home, he went to college on the GI Bill, which made it possible for him and so many veterans like him to live out their own version of the American Dream. And now it's our turn to help guarantee this generation the same opportunity that the greatest generation enjoyed by providing every returning service member with a real chance to afford a college education. And by providing the resources to effectively implement the Post-9/11 GI Bill, that is what this budget does.

And even as we care for veterans who've served this country, Bob Gates has helped us design a budget that does more for our soldiers, more for their families, and more for our military. It fully protects and properly funds the increase to our Army and Marine force strength and halts reductions in the Air Force and Navy, allowing fewer deployments and more time between each. It builds on care for our wounded warriors and on our investments in medical research and development. It deepens our commitment to improve the quality of life for military families—military child care, spousal support, and education—because they're deployed when their loved one gets deployed.

On my visit to Baghdad this week, I was inspired all over again by the men and women in our armed services. They're proud of the work they're doing. And we are all deeply proud of them. And through their service, they are living out the ideals that stir something deep within the American character—honor, sacrifice, and commitment to a higher purpose and to one another.

That, after all, is what led them to wear the uniform in the first place—their unwavering belief in America. And now we must serve them as well as they've served us. And as long as we are fortunate to have leaders like Secretary Gates and Secretary Shinseki, and as long as I am Commander-in-Chief, I promise that we will work tirelessly to meet that mission and make sure that all those who wear this nation's uniform know this: When you come home to America, America will be there for you.

5

Veterans' Health Care Is a Massive Unfunded Liability

Kelley B. Vlahos

Kelley B. Vlahos is a Washington, D.C.-based writer. She has worked for FoxNews.com and Homeland Security Today *magazine, and has been a contributing editor for* The American Conservative.

Members of the US Congress appear to be indifferent to the massive costs that are being incurred as a result of the wars in Iraq and Afghanistan. Millions of Americans have served in these conflicts, and future health care and disability costs alone are projected to be nearly $1 trillion. The costs of the wars are too high, and it is time to bring the conflict to an end so resources can be directed to veterans who need them.

Experts say the projected cost of the wars in Iraq and Afghanistan has gone up another trillion dollars, but the general sound we hear from Congress isn't outrage. More likely it's the sound of crickets.

Crickets most definitely from the empty chairs at the House Veterans Affairs Committee, a clear majority of which didn't bother to show up Thursday [September 30, 2010] for a full panel meeting on Capitol Hill regarding the "True Cost of War." Granted, Congress had just adjourned until mid-November that morning, and most members had one foot out the door before 10 a.m., itching hard to hit the campaign trail in their home districts. They do have priorities, you know.

You could practically count the number of members who bothered to show up on one hand, and they were all Democrats. Three congressmen not on the committee sat in, including Rep. Walter Jones (R-N.C.), one of the few GOP war critics in Congress, who sat noticeably in front of 25 empty committee seats. But within an hour or so, all were gone but Chairman Bob Filner (D-Calif.), looking lonely across from the sizable (but definitely not standing room only) audience of mostly veterans' advocates all too used to the feeling of talking to a wall.

The media presence also appeared close to nil—save for me and another guy at the end of a very long, empty table, and perhaps one blogger somewhere in the crowd.

As of March [2010], more than 565,000 [Iraq and Afghanistan War] veterans have already been treated by the VA. They hadn't expected to reach that number until 2016.

The hearing certainly didn't generate the atmospheric drama as say, a Hill visit by Stephen Colbert, but testimony by the morning's key witnesses was dramatic, if not foreboding, and much more critical than much of the hoo-hah that passes for "the people's business" in Congress these days.

According to researchers Joseph Stiglitz and Linda Bilmes, authors of *The Three Trillion Dollar War*, their 2008 estimates for the long-term cost of the wars in Iraq and Afghanistan were *too conservative*; in fact, they were way off. They pointed specifically to the cost of veterans' care, which they revised up from $717 billion to $934 billion—nearly $1 trillion in health and disability costs alone!

Why? Stiglitz and Bilmes estimated two years ago that 30 to 33 percent of returning Iraq and Afghanistan war veterans (fewer than 400,000) would have sought care in the Veterans Administration (VA) health system by 2010. But as of March, more than 565,000 such veterans have already been treated by the VA. They hadn't expected to reach that number until 2016.

And that figure is likely much higher today. According to Paul Sullivan, director of Veterans for Common Sense (VCS), new patients average some 9,000 a month. Taking that into account, there could be closer to 620,000 new vets in the system today.

Estimates Are Staggering

As a result, estimates for long-term medical care were revised up from $284 billion to $348 billion.

Meanwhile, Stiglitz and Bilmes estimated two years ago that between 366,000 and 398,000 returning vets would have filed disability compensation (cash) claims by 2010, when in fact, more than 518,000 have already filed such claims. So, the researchers revised their estimates for long-term disability costs from $388 billion to $534 billion.

Furthermore, estimates for disability payments through Social Security went from $43 billion to $52 billion.

This is just a snapshot of course. These figures, Stiglitz and Bilmes point out, do not include costs to Medicare or military TRICARE for Life or active duty health care spending, which has gone up a staggering 167 percent since 2001. They don't include vet-related costs to state and local governments, the GI Bill, home loan guarantees, job training services, and expanding VA facilities and programs due to increased demands.

Bottom line, 2008 estimates for the costliest of veterans' care—medical, disability and Social Security payments—had to be revised up *25 percent* based on current trends, said Stiglitz, a 2000 Nobel Memorial Prize winner. "The new book should be called the 'Four to Six Trillion Dollar War and Increasing,'" he told the committee. "We will be getting a full assemblage of numbers in January. What is clear . . . the total cost is substantially higher."

Such news should have the effect of a bugle blast on the Congress. Or at least induce queasiness, suggested Winslow Wheeler, budget analyst for the Center for Defense Information.

One would think . . . there might be a much broader discussion over whether our increasingly unpopular wars are worth the cost.

"When Bilmes and Stiglitz originally estimated the cost of the $3 trillion dollar war, everybody gagged, especially the advocates who said the war would be near 'self-financing,'" he told Antiwar.com. "Now, they need to gag a little harder. We should too."

Ignorance Prevails

One would think that for all of the marching, praying and campaigning against unwieldy federal spending and the debt, there might be a much broader discussion over whether our increasingly unpopular wars are worth the cost.

Ignorance is prevailing instead, said Filner. "It's like looking at the homeless, no one wants to look at it. I don't think Americans want to know the true cost of war."

Members of Congress certainly have a hard time with it. Filner noted that Congress is just getting down to compensating World War II vets caught up in atomic testing and Vietnam veterans suffering from the effects of Agent Orange. "This is a disgrace . . . an abrogation of our fundamental responsibility as a Congress," he said, noting "the system we have makes it much easier to send our troops into harm's way . . . than to care for them when they get home."

In their original report, Stiglitz, an economist at Columbia University, and Bilmes, who teaches public policy at the Kennedy School of Government at Harvard University, assessed the long-term costs of the war based on operations continuing through 2017. They did this in an attempt to show the American public that aside from the Goliath budget for the Department of Defense—$680 billion for fiscal year 2010 alone—and the terribly expensive operational costs of the war—more than $1 trillion since 2001—there are a range of long-term hidden and often overlooked costs like veterans' care, and the economic and social costs of the war.

"Long-term veterans' costs as they are now are beginning to approach the cost of what we spend in actual combat operations," said Bilmes. "We know at least at the minimum, the veterans' costs will be higher than what we expected."

Over the last nine years, more than 2.1 million Americans have served more than three million tours of duty and 1.25 million veterans have returned home. Long-term costs of the Iraq and Afghanistan conflicts can be expected to be higher than previous conflicts because of 1) higher survival rates for injured soldiers, 2) higher instances of Post Traumatic Disorder (PTSD) and other mental health ailments, 3) more vets applying for benefits and 4) more generous benefits over all, Stiglitz and Bilmes told the committee.

Here's is some language that the Tea Partiers—none of which, by the way, were pressing into the Veterans' Affairs Committee room Thursday—might understand. According to the Stiglitz-Bilmes team, "the U.S. debt rose from $6.5 trillion to $10 trillion between 2003 and 2008, before the financial crisis. At least one-fourth of that debt is directly attributable to the wars," and that doesn't include the "unfunded liabilities" wrapped up in caring for veterans.

One Man's Story

That would include someone like Robert Warren, 20, who is recovering from a bomb blast he survived in Afghanistan in May, shortly after he arrived in-country. According to a *Washington Post* feature on Sunday, Warren has a piece of shrapnel in his carotid artery and a large portion of his skull removed by doctors so that he might survive. He has severe brain injuries that affect his long-term memory and other cognitive skills. He has years of rehabilitation ahead of him; he just became a father.

The scale of our financial commitment to providing for veterans is huge ... but at present, the U.S. has no provision for how it will pay for this long-term liability.

Warren joins the rest of the 20 percent of service members who are estimated to have incurred some level of traumatic brain injury (TBI) on the battlefield and survived. The "signature wound" of the current war, science is still trying to catch up with the how to best diagnose TBI, how to heal it, and how to integrate soldiers back into their lives while they are forced to live with it. And it is expensive, according to lawmakers present at Thursday's hearing—Congress has already approved $1.2 billion in TBI-related funding. Next month, according to the *Post*, the National Naval Medical Center in Bethesda will open a $65 million TBI unit, which will only be able to care for 20 severely damaged individuals at a time.

And the injuries keep coming. According to Sullivan at VCS, a total of 92,384 servicemembers have been wounded or were medically evacuated due to injury or illness since the war began. And it will certainly increase, with 100,000 troops in Afghanistan and 50,000 still in Iraq today.

"The scale of our financial commitment to providing for veterans is huge," said Stiglitz and Bilmes. "But at present, the U.S. has no provision for how it will pay for this long-term liability."

The Future Is Uncertain

Several Democrats have thought this through before. They think that if the country is going to send its men and women off to a bloody war, it should at least be able to pay for it. The

"Share the Sacrifice Act," which would incorporate a temporary tax to offset the costs of the war, has seen different incarnations, but has so far failed to get off the ground, mainly because Republicans see it as a Democratic ploy to end the war and most Democrats are too scared to push it.

So now Filner says he will be proposing a "Veterans Trust Fund," to be paid for with a "surcharge," dedicated to ensuring these astronomical costs will be paid, despite hard times and changing political winds. One veterans' advocate sitting in the audience Thursday pointed out that while Congress has indeed been attentive to their needs—VA appropriations have increased from $90 billion to $125 billion in the last four years—there is no guarantee that a shift in party control this November won't give way to "extremists that want to cut back and then privatize VA under the smokescreen of cutting the debt."

Here's an idea—how about ending the wars? Several (failed) attempts were made in July by members to start withdrawing troops now (instead of 2011—what's the difference?). Most "experts" are increasingly framing operations in Afghanistan as hopeless, and with [Islamic political leader] Muqtada al Sadr on the ascent in Iraq, we're likely not too long for that place either. Why not save a few skulls (and a lot more money) in the meantime? Then we can concentrate on the billions in lifetime costs we're already obligated to pay.

If a kid repeatedly broke his bones climbing trees, his father wouldn't take on a part-time job just to pay for the medical bills, he would tell the kid to stop climbing the damn trees and come home.

We need to get our men and women out of the trees and back home, and then we can start the healing.

6

Veterans Administration Health Care Is Not Readily Available in Rural Areas

Associated Press

The Associated Press is a global news network with headquarters in New York.

More than one third of the veterans of Iraq and Afghanistan who are enrolled for Veterans Administration (VA) health care live in rural areas. Often, veterans from rural areas choose not to enroll for benefits they have earned because of the distances— sometimes hundreds of miles—involved in visiting a Department of Veterans Affairs Hospital. The VA's Office of the Inspector General recently determined that the VA is not able to account for $273 million in funding that was intended to improve access and quality of care for veterans living in rural areas. Additionally, the agency lost a court case filed by veterans who claimed that it delayed and denied care to former service members suffering from post-traumatic stress disorder, traumatic brain injury, and mental health issues. In response to these events, the VA has increased efforts to improve the care that is available for rural veterans.

Frank Munk earned his veteran's medical benefits more than four decades ago in Quang Tri province, a hard-fought, bloody piece of ground in Vietnam. Yet he doesn't always choose to use them.

Associated Press, "For Veterans in Rural Areas, Health Care Can Be a Battle," *STLToday .com*, June 2011. © 2011 by Associated Press. All rights reserved. Reproduced by permission.

Munk, 64, a truck mechanic from western Kansas, instead spends $2,500 out of his own pocket on a private doctor for such things as hearing tests. It's either that or drive nearly 300 miles to a Department of Veterans Affairs hospital in Wichita or Denver.

"I can't afford to take two days off," said Munk, who's self-employed. "The VA care is getting cost-prohibitive for people in the rural areas because of the time, and a lot of them can't drive themselves."

Long Distances Are a Problem for Many Veterans

Other veterans who live beyond America's cities and suburbs share Munk's dilemma. Long distances and restrictive rules have become obstacles to health care for many of the more than 3 million rural veterans enrolled in the VA health system. They account for 41 percent of enrollees.

But the agency's effort to aid rural veterans has other problems as well. An April internal VA audit found that it couldn't determine whether much of the money spent on rural health care in recent years did any good.

The VA Office of Rural Health did an inadequate job of assessing the health care needs of rural veterans and managing the money for expanding care.

The VA Office of Inspector General, the agency's internal watchdog, concluded that the VA "lacked reasonable assurance" that its use of $273 million of the $533 million in rural health funding it received in 2009 and 2010 had "improved access and quality of care" for veterans.

"We basically couldn't tell how effective each of these projects was because of the lack of project performance measures," said Gary Abe, a director in the inspector general's office who oversaw the audit. "The report's message was the VA couldn't determine if it was money well spent."

The report noted that the VA Office of Rural Health did an inadequate job of assessing the health care needs of rural veterans and managing the money for expanding care. In addition, oversight of rural health care programs was ineffective, and communication with other agencies and services involved in rural care was poor, it said.

Committed to Expanding Access

VA officials agreed with the report's recommendations for improving the rural health program, including the use of financial controls to check spending. VA spokesman Josh Taylor said the department was committed to expanding access to rural veterans.

"We take very seriously our responsibility to ensure veterans receive the health care and benefits they have earned." he said.

Democratic Sen. Patty Murray of Washington, the chairman of the Senate Veterans' Affairs Committee, said the inspector general's report was worrisome.

Indeed, suicides among Iraq and Afghanistan veterans have reached record levels.

"At a time when we have to fight for every dollar our veterans get, it is unacceptable that VA can't say whether hundreds of millions of dollars spent to improve health care for rural veterans had any impact on improving access or quality," she said.

System Under Stress

Although there appears to be general agreement that VA hospitals provide good medical care, the system has been under extreme stress because of the wars in Iraq and Afghanistan.

Few expected that the wars would last so long, or planned for the flood of patients or the severity of their injuries. VA officials are trying to manage a generation of combat veterans who have come home bearing not only the deep physical scars of battle but invisible psychological wounds as well that will require years—if not a lifetime, in many cases—of care.

Indeed, suicides among Iraq and Afghanistan veterans have reached record levels.

The VA recently lost a two-year court battle against two veterans groups that had sued the agency over its delay and denial of mental health care and benefits for former service members suffering from post-traumatic stress disorder [PTSD], traumatic brain injury and other psychological problems.

One Out of Every Three

Rural America is home to more than a third of the Iraq and Afghanistan veterans who are enrolled in the VA; not all have combat-related health problems. But the VA has stepped up efforts to reach out to rural veterans from all eras.

Telemedicine—in which patients are diagnosed and treated via electronic communication—is one way that veterans can get treatment at home. A network of about 800 community-based outpatient clinics that provides rural veterans with basic medical care such as checkups, X-rays and prescriptions is another.

"It's an attempt to cut costs," said Lana McKenzie, the director of medical services for Paralyzed Veterans of America, a veterans service group. "If you are a healthy vet and ambulatory and live in the area, and need insulin or blood pressure medicine, it works. But it doesn't work if you get further complicated than that."

Out-of-Network Options Are Lacking

In general, the VA won't pay for a veteran to see an out-of-network doctor if the same care is available within the system—even if it's more convenient.

Frank Di Piano, 33, an ex-Marine and Iraq veteran who lives near Springfield, Mo., suffered traumatic brain injury after a mortar exploded outside a command tent in Ramadi in 2004. He also has a bad shoulder injury from boot camp that never healed properly.

He drives nearly 300 miles every few weeks to the VA medical center in Oklahoma City to see doctors about his shoulder. It initially took him six months to schedule an MRI.

He also regularly makes the 130-mile trip to the VA hospital in Fayetteville, Ark., for treatment for PTSD.

Di Piano said some physicians he knew had told him that he could get the same care for his shoulder at a hospital in Springfield if the VA would allow him to go outside the network. So he asked.

"They said they couldn't get authorization to do that because it was just too much red tape," Di Piano said.

7

The Government Aims to Improve Health Care Access for Rural Veterans

United States Department of Veterans Affairs

The Department of Veterans Affairs is responsible for administering health care and other benefits to retired service members and their families.

Many veterans of the wars in Iraq and Afghanistan live in rural areas of the country where access to health care, including the health care services of the Department of Veterans Affairs, is limited. The Veterans Administration created the Office of Rural Health to improve the availability of health care services for rural veterans.

*M*ission—The mission of (ORH) [Office of Rural Health] is to improve access and quality of care for enrolled rural and highly rural Veterans by developing evidence-based policies and innovative practices to support the unique needs of enrolled Veterans residing in geographically remote areas.

Background—About 3.3 million Veterans (41% of total) enrolled in the Department of Veterans Affairs (VA) Health Care System live in rural or highly rural areas of the country. These Veterans make up a disproportionate share of service members and comprise about 39% of the enrolled Veterans who served in Iraq and Afghanistan, many of whom are returning to their rural communities.

United States Department of Veterans Affairs, "About the Office of Rural Health," June 8, 2011. www.ruralhealth.va.gov.

In order to better serve rural Veterans, the VA created the Office of Rural Health in 2007. Located in the Office of the Assistant Deputy Undersecretary for Policy and Planning of the Veterans Health Administration (VHA), the mission of ORH is to improve access and quality of health care for all Veterans through a combination of community based clinic expansion, increased partnerships with non-VA rural providers, increased use of telemedicine and information technology and a new effort to recruit and retain health care providers to rural areas.

Individuals living in rural areas have traditionally been underserved with regard to health care access.

The Structure of the Office of Rural Health

The Office of Rural Health is headquartered in Washington, DC. It is organizationally located in the VHA Office of the Assistant Deputy Under Secretary for Policy and Planning. Director Mary Beth Skupien, PhD and Deputy Director Sheila Warren, MPH, RN, CPHQ along with their staff, both at headquarters and in the field, direct National ORH activities and communications as well as oversee the budget and performance of all ORH-funded programs across the VA system.

Individuals living in rural areas have traditionally been underserved with regard to health care access. The reasons for this are multiple and varied, but mainly stem from the need to travel long distances to health care facilities, lack of health insurance, lack of specialized care and an inadequate number of health care providers working in rural areas. As a result, rural populations tend to be in poorer health; in fact, a study by the Office of Health and Human services estimates that half of the adults living in rural areas suffer from a chronic health condition. With regard to rural Veterans, there are the additional health complications associated with combat exposure such as PTSD [post-traumatic stress disorder], depression, and traumatic brain injury.

Veterans Rural Health Resource Center-Eastern Region (VRHRC-ER)—The Eastern Region Center is located in three different VA medical centers: Gainesville, FL; Togus, ME; and White River Junction, VT and is currently under the direction of Dr. Paul Hoffman. The work of the VRHRC-ER has been focused on the education and training of VA and non-VA service providers caring for rural Veterans and bringing specialty care to community-based clinics via telehealth technology.

Veterans Rural Health Resource Center-Central Region (VRHRC-CR)—The Central Region Center, based at the VA medical center in Iowa City, IA, is under the direction of Dr. Peter Kaboli. This center's work has been focused on evaluating existing rural health clinical programs and testing of novel strategies to overcome barriers to access and quality.

Veterans Rural Health Resource Center-Western Region (VRHRC-WR)—The Western Region Center, under the direction of Dr. Byron Bair, is located at the VA medical center in Salt Lake City. Their current work is focused on improving access to care for rural Native Veterans through outreach activities, piloting of best care models and deployment of telemental health. In addition, they are focusing on the care of rural, elderly Veterans through the development of a web-based tool kit designed to support their caregivers.

VISN [Veterans Integrated Service Network] Rural Consultants—Each VISN has either a full or part-time rural consultant (VRC) whose main functions are to enhance service delivery to Veterans residing in rural and highly rural areas, and to facilitate information exchange and learning within and across each VISN, as well as support a stronger link between ORH and each VISN. In practical terms, the VRCs work closely with internal and external stakeholders in their respective VISNs to introduce, implement and evaluate ORH-funded projects, as well as monitor the budget and report on the effectiveness of each. In addition, VRCs conduct outreach to develop strong relationships with the community, including State Offices of Rural Health, local health care providers, advocacy groups, Veterans groups and academic institutions. Further, each VRC is responsible for the development of a rural strategic plan that must incorporate outcomes of periodic needs assessment for their respective VISN.

Veterans Rural Health Advisory Committee

The Veterans Rural Health Advisory Committee (VRHAC) consists of 12 members, appointed by former VA Secretary Dr. James B. Peake. The VRHAC is tasked with examining ways to enhance health care services for Veterans in rural areas. The committee, chaired by James F. Ahrens, former head of the Montana Hospital Association, includes Veterans; rural health experts in academia; state and Federal rural health professionals; state-level Department of Veterans Affairs officials; and leaders of Veterans Service Organizations. The VRHAC hosts a minimum of two face-to-face meetings a year and provides a written summary of committee activities to the VA Secretary on an annual basis.

8

The Veterans Administration Does Not Provide Proper Services for PTSD

Carol J. Williams

Carol J. Williams is an award-winning reporter who has worked for the Los Angeles Times *for more than 20 years. She wrote this article while assigned to cover legal affairs for the* Los Angeles Times Metro *staff.*

In May 2011 a federal appeals court ruled that the Department of Veterans Affairs has violated the rights of many US service veterans by failing to provide timely health care for those who are suffering from post-traumatic stress disorder. Treatment of war wounds is guaranteed by law for 25 million veterans in the US, including 1.6 million who have served in Iraq and Afghanistan in recent years.

A federal appeals court Tuesday [May 10, 2011] lambasted the Department of Veterans Affairs for failing to care for those suffering post-traumatic stress disorder [PTSD] and ordered a major overhaul of the behemoth agency.

Treatment delays for PTSD and other combat-related mental illnesses are so "egregious" that they violate veterans' constitutional rights and contribute to the despair behind many of the 6,500 suicides among veterans each year, the U.S. 9th Circuit Court of Appeals said in its 2-1 ruling.

Noting that an average of 18 returning service members commit suicide each day, the court directed a district judge in San Francisco to order sweeping reform of the VA's mental healthcare system.

The appeals court took nearly two years to issue its decision, in part because the court attempted to force the government to negotiate with the two veterans' groups that sued over mental health care and benefits that had been delayed or denied.

Attempts at Mediation Only Led to Deadlock

Citing the court's inability to order the government "to work faster," Chief Judge Alex Kozinski had urged lawyers for the VA and the veterans groups to use the court's mediation services to work out a plan for meeting the wounded veterans' needs. The talks deadlocked and no settlement was reached.

The VA's unchecked incompetence has gone on long enough; no more veterans should be compelled to agonize or perish while the government fails to perform its obligations.

"There comes a time when the political branches have so completely and chronically failed to respect the People's constitutional rights that the courts must be willing to enforce them. We have reached that unfortunate point with respect to veterans who are suffering from the hidden, or not hidden, wounds of war," said the ruling written by Judge Stephen Reinhardt and joined by Senior Judge Procter Hug Jr., both appointees of President Carter.

"The VA's unchecked incompetence has gone on long enough; no more veterans should be compelled to agonize or perish while the government fails to perform its obligations," the ruling said.

Kozinski dissented, saying that "much as the VA's failure to meet the needs of veterans with PTSD might shock and outrage us, we may not step in and boss it around."

He predicted that the majority's directive would only prolong litigation and complicate the agency's efforts to improve services.

Congress or the President Should Have Acted

"We would have preferred Congress or the President to have remedied the VA's egregious problems without our intervention when evidence of the department's harmful shortcomings and its failure to properly address the needs of our veterans first came to light years ago," the majority said in heeding the chief judge's concerns.

Veterans for Common Sense and Veterans United for Truth sued the VA four years ago, alleging systemic failures in the government's processing of disability claims and appeals of denied coverage. U.S. District Judge Samuel Conti denied the groups' claims on procedural grounds following a seven-day trial in 2008. The judge said he lacked the authority to order the VA to implement the Mental Health Strategic Plan it drafted in 2004 to overhaul its care system within five years.

Gordon Erspamer, the San Francisco attorney who represented the veterans groups pro bono, said he provided Conti three years ago with remedial plans for the VA to improve services to veterans, proposing firm deadlines for dealing with treatment requests and benefit claims. He said he was concerned, though, that the government would continue to appeal the case, further delaying the needed reforms.

"We're not dealing with the rights of convicted criminals here, or the rights of foreign combatants. We're dealing with our people, our veterans. It's a tough issue to be so inflexible on," he said of the federal government's resistance to direction from the courts.

Charles S. Miller, a spokesman for the Justice Department whose lawyers argued the case in defense of the VA, said the department had no immediate comment except to say that it was reviewing the 9th Circuit ruling.

Treatment of war wounds has been a legal guarantee to soldiers since Abraham Lincoln was president, and the law was enhanced in 1998 to promise free care for "any medical condition, even if the condition is not attributable to military service."

The VA is obliged to provide a mental health assessment within 30 days for any veteran requesting help, but . . . many applications languish for months or years . . . because of chronic shortages.

PTSD Is Widespread

Tuesday's ruling noted that there are 25 million veterans in the United States, including 1.6 million who served in Iraq or Afghanistan over the past decade.

"PTSD is a leading mental health disorder diagnosis for those veterans," the appeals panel said, citing a Rand Institute study in 2008 estimating that 300,000 returning war veterans currently suffer from PTSD or major depression.

The VA is obliged to provide a mental health assessment within 30 days for any veteran requesting help, but many applications languish for months or years, and tens of thousands of those deemed in need of care are relegated to waiting lists because of chronic shortages, the judges noted.

The ruling also cited a 2007 report by the Office of the Inspector General that there were no suicide prevention officers at any of the VA's 800 community-based outpatient clinics, where most veterans receive their medical care.

9

Many Veterans Struggle to Heal from Moral Injuries

Diane Silver

Diane Silver is a journalist whose work has appeared at Salon
.com, *in* The Progressive, Ms. Magazine, *and in daily newspapers across the country. She blogs at www.InSearchOfGoodness
.com.*

*Suicide rates in the military are a serious problem, and it is now
recognized that many returning veterans suffer with major depression. Researchers in the Department of Veterans Affairs, as
well as in private groups that work with veterans, are increasingly finding it necessary to address the spiritual as well as the
emotional dimensions of post-traumatic stress disorder. The concept of moral injury has proven helpful in many cases, as a way
of describing deep yet invisible wounds that some combat veterans have experienced.*

John Fisher got his soul back when he visited a cemetery in
Greece.

Shelley Corteville felt "rocketed" into healing when she
told her story at a veterans' retreat after 28 years of silence.

Bob Cagle lost his decades-long urge to commit suicide after an encounter at a Buddhist temple.

These veterans and thousands like them grapple with what
some call "the war after the war"—the psychological scars of
conflict. Working with the U.S. Department of Veterans Af-

fairs and private organizations, these men and women are employing treatments both radically new and centuries old. At the center of their journey is a new way of thinking that redefines some traumas as moral injuries.

The psychological toll taken by war is obvious. For the second year in a row, more active-duty troops committed suicide in 2010 (468) than were killed in combat in Iraq and Afghanistan (462). A 2008 RAND Corporation study reported that nearly 1 in 5 troops who had returned from Iraq and Afghanistan reported symptoms of post-traumatic stress or major depression.

What sometimes happens in war may more accurately be called a moral injury—a deep soul wound that pierces a person's identity, sense of morality and relationship to society.

A Wounded Identity

Since the American Psychiatric Association added post-traumatic stress disorder, or PTSD, to its diagnostic manual in 1980, the diagnosis has most often focused on trauma associated with threats *to* a soldier's life. Today, however, therapists such as Jonathan Shay, a retired VA psychiatrist and recipient of a MacArthur Foundation "genius" grant; Edward Tick, director of the private group Soldier's Heart; and Brett Litz, a VA psychologist, argue that this concept is too limited. What sometimes happens in war may more accurately be called a moral injury—a deep soul wound that pierces a person's identity, sense of morality and relationship to society. In short, a threat *in* a solder's life.

"My colleagues and I suspect that the greatest lasting harm is from moral injury," says Litz, director of the Mental Health Core of the Massachusetts Veterans Epidemiological Research and Information Center. He and six colleagues published an article on the topic in the December 2009 *Clinical Psychological Review*, in which they define moral injury as a wound that can occur when troops participate in, witness or fall victim to actions that transgress their most deeply held moral beliefs.

A Controversial Idea

While the severity of this kind of wound differs from person to person, moral injury can lead to deep despair.

"They have lost their sense that virtue is even possible," Shay says. "It corrodes the soul."

Litz acknowledges that the idea of moral injury is "controversial and provocative." Neither the military, VA nor the American Psychiatric Association have sanctioned this as a diagnosis, but the concept is gaining traction. In April, psychologists, officers and chaplains led a plenary session on the topic at the Navy and Marine Corps Combat and Operational Stress Control Conference in San Diego.

In Europe, post-traumatic stress disorder researcher Ulrike Schmidt even seeks evidence of the moral injury in brain tissue itself. As she told Miller-McCune.com recently, "They need to know that it's a recognized disorder. They are not weak, they're sick, they have a spiritual wound. . . . And it's important that they aren't treated like outsiders, which is how many soldiers were treated in Europe in the '40s and '50s."

Self-Indictment

Georgetown University ethics professor Nancy Sherman heard stories of moral trauma when she interviewed veterans of Iraq, Afghanistan, Vietnam and World War II for her 2010 book, *The Untold War*. "It might be where you felt you should have been able to do more for your buddies, but you couldn't, or because you simply survived," she says.

"Regret," she writes, "doesn't begin to capture what the soldiers I talked with feel. It doesn't capture the despair or depth of the feeling—the awful weight of self-indictment and the need to make moral repair in order to be allowed back into the community in which he feels he has somehow jeopardized his standing."

Vietnam veterans John Fisher and Bob Cagle know that weight. Fisher served as a forward artillery observer and assistant gunner in 1968 and 1969. He vividly remembers the first time he shot an enemy soldier.

"I realized that I had taken his soul away from him," Fisher says. "In the process, my soul was gone."

Cagle served as an infantryman from 1965 to 1966. When he first killed a soldier in combat, he immediately thought of the commandment: "Thou shalt not kill."

"Well, I guess I screwed that up," Cagle told himself at the time. "God will never forgive me."

When Cagle saw the body and realized that his enemy looked no older than 14, his guilt deepened. "He would have shot me in a heartbeat, I had no doubt, but I just couldn't get over that."

Moral injury does not always occur on a battlefield.

Forgiveness Is a Problem

Fisher and Cagle came home to thoughts of suicide. "I literally couldn't condone any of the things I had to participate in to save my own life," Fisher says.

Although both eventually found successful careers (Fisher as a chiropractor and Cagle as a respiratory therapist), they struggled, enduring failed marriages, flashbacks and fits of anger and anxiety.

Moral injury does not always occur on a battlefield. In more than 20 years of treating veterans, MacArthur Fellow Shay concluded that these wounds most often occur when leaders betray soldiers in high-stakes situations, whether or not that occurs in combat.

Shelley Corteville, for example, was an Army air traffic controller from 1978 to 1980 in South Korea, where she was raped five times by a fellow soldier. The fault, she thought, was her own. After all, other soldiers and officers constantly referred to women as "whores or tramps" who were always "asking for it." She did not believe these same officers would punish a rapist, so she kept silent, working side-by-side with the man every day.

After leaving the Army, Corteville drank heavily, married and divorced repeatedly. She moved 58 times and worked at 29 different jobs.

"Everything Lightened"

Therapists have devised a variety of treatments. Litz and his colleagues represent a traditional approach, using a modified talk therapy where a patient interacts with a therapist in an office. Their approach includes creating a bond between the patient and a therapist who can accept unconditionally and listen "without revulsion." Therapists also guide patients through an imaginary dialogue with a "benevolent moral authority" and help them plan practical tasks to make amends.

Litz and his colleagues tested their therapeutic strategy on 25 active-duty Marines in a pilot project. This summer, they launched a four-year study with 300 Marines struggling with moral injury and other psychological problems.

"In traditional cultures, warriors always came back to tell their stories, to give witness and to do healing ceremonies in front of the entire community."

Tick represents a different approach. He sees talk therapy as a dead end. "We can only do so much review and expression and catharsis and processing," he says. "That's all wonderful and necessary, but combat veterans who have participated in destroying the world can be stuck in their grief and in their identity of being a destroyer."

He uses groups where veterans share experiences, but he also turns to ritual, charity work, visits to former battlefields and even a redefinition of what it means to be a soldier.

Tick, his wife and co-director, Kate Dahlstedt, and a tiny staff at the nonprofit Soldier's Heart in Troy, N.Y., have worked with several hundred people, including active-duty service members and veterans of Iraq and Afghanistan. At the core of their approach is a redefinition of soldiering based on Tick's research into warrior traditions as discussed in his 2005 book *War and the Soul*.

A Burden the Whole Community Shares

"In traditional cultures, warriors always came back to tell their stories, to give witness and to do healing ceremonies in front of the entire community," Tick says. "The community witnessed the stories, felt the emotions, carried the burdens with their warriors and transferred responsibility for actions from the warriors to the community."

Today, Tick, and veterans and civilians inspired by his book, are attempting to re-create some of those experiences from the past. Volunteer groups in 18 U.S. cities, Canada and Vietnam hold listening circles, where veterans share stories with each other and civilians, and veterans mentor each other. Tick also leads trips to ancient and modern battlefields.

No in-depth data yet exists on the effectiveness of any form of treatment for moral injury. Litz's study is the first large-scale effort to do that; he says some of Tick's methods "make sense conceptually," but he will not comment further without seeing data. So far, most of the evaluation of Tick's results has been anecdotal.

Fisher, Cagle and Corteville have all worked with Soldier's Heart.

Corteville, 51, of Springfield, Ore., went to her first retreat in 2009. She had already been through five years of counseling with the VA and been sober for 17 years. "In all that time, I still hadn't dealt with my PTSD," she says.

At the retreat, Corteville finally talked about being raped. "That very first retreat is what rocketed me into healing." As a result, she left a failing marriage and is working on a degree in sociology.

Fisher, 63, of Murrells Inlet, S.C., contacted Tick after reading his book. Despite years of therapy, Fisher was still "waking up in the middle of the night screaming." Fisher's breakthrough came when he accompanied Tick to Greece, and they visited the Kerameikos cemetery.

Fisher sat on a knoll and listened as Tick read an oration for the war dead that had been delivered on the same spot 2,500 years before. Fisher says he felt like he was floating, and he realized that his soul, his sense of self, had fled his body while he was in Vietnam. "My heart felt like it was dark inside before. Now it felt like someone had turned on the light."

Journeys in Search of Healing

Fisher returned home and ended a bad marriage. Today, he leads Soldier's Heart trips to Vietnam, where veterans meet former foes and conduct charity projects.

Cagle, 65, of Atlanta, views healing as a process. For him, the most useful activity has been writing about his experiences. But the turning point came when he returned to Vietnam with Tick. At first, the trip was a nightmare, as Cagle suffered constant flashbacks and saw visions of the young soldier he had killed. Eventually, the group climbed to a Buddhist temple on a mountain. While the others took off their shoes, Cagle looked up and saw the boy.

"I don't even know how to describe it." Cagle struggles to speak as he retells the story. "I'm trying to get my voice back." He pauses. "Ed [Tick] came over and said, 'Let's go on in.'

"I said, 'You don't see him, do you?'

"Ed said, 'Who?'

"I said, 'That's the boy I shot.'

"Ed said, 'What's going on?'

"I said, 'I think we're talking to one another on some level I don't get.'"

Cagle says he felt a crushing weight slip off his shoulders. "From then on, my whole everything lightened. I felt relieved. I felt like this kid could finally go wherever he was supposed to go. That's when I really started healing."

Today, Cagle helps run Veterans Heart Georgia. Healing takes time, but it is possible, he says.

"It's not a group of 500 people getting together and having some great epiphany. It's a one-on-one process. It's people who care about one another, who are trying to heal themselves and others."

10

The Veterans Administration Is Committed to the Needs of Women Veterans

Patricia Hayes

Patricia Hayes is a Chief Consultant to the Women Veterans Health Strategic Health Care Group of the Department of Veterans Affairs.

The number of women veterans is growing. Of the 1.8 million women veterans in the US, more than 450,000 have enrolled for health care services through the Veterans Administration (VA). They deserve care of the highest quality. However, the recent increase in numbers of women veterans has placed a strain on the system, and is challenging the VA to develop more effective policies and practices for providing health care for women, in order to achieve the same level of care available to male veterans.

Good morning, Mr. Chairman and Ranking Member. Thank you for the opportunity to discuss how the Department of Veterans Affairs' (VA) has provided, and will continue to improve, health care availability for women Veterans. I would like to thank the Chair, this Committee and Senator Murray specifically for your interest in working with VA to ensure women Veterans receive the care they have earned through service to their country.

The Secretary has recently testified before this Committee that enhancing primary care for women Veterans is one of

Patricia Hayes, "Testimony to Senate Committee on Veterans Affairs." veterans.senate .gov, July 14, 2009.

VA's top priorities. VA recognizes that the number of women Veterans is growing with women becoming increasingly dependent on VA for their health care. Of the 1.8 million women Veterans in the United States more than 450,000 have enrolled for care. This number is expected to grow by 30 percent in the next 5 years. Women currently comprise approximately 14 percent of the active duty military, 17.6 percent of Guard and Reserves and 5.9 percent of VA health care users.

Women who were deployed and served in the recent conflicts in Afghanistan and Iraq are enrolling in VA at historical rates. Of all women who were deployed and served in Afghanistan or Iraq, 44 percent have enrolled and 43 percent have used VA between 2 and 11 times. This suggests that many of our newer women Veterans rely more heavily on VA to meet their health care needs. . . .

The VA Faces New Challenges

Women Veterans entering VA's system are younger and have health care needs distinct from their male counterparts. The average age of women Veterans is 48 years old, compared to 61 years old among men. Nearly all newly enrolled women Veterans accessing VA care are under 40 and of childbearing age. This trend creates a need to shift how we provide health care.

General primary care and gender-specific care needs of women Veterans are currently provided through a multi-visit, multi-provider model that may not achieve the continuity of care desired. Additionally, some VA facilities rely on outside providers for gender-specific primary care and specialty gynecological care through the use of fee-basis care. This approach to women's health delivery can provide challenges in providing continuity of care.

Moving to a more comprehensive primary care delivery model could challenge VA clinicians, who may have dealt predominately with male Veterans and sometimes have little or no exposure to female patients. VA facilities may also need to increase both focus and resources on women's health (e.g., space, staffing, appropriately equipped exam rooms) to ensure adequate privacy for women during examinations. Initiatives are underway and under development to address these and other changes brought on by the increasing number of women Veterans seeking care from VA.

Some women report that lack of newborn care and child care forces them to seek care elsewhere.

The Quality of Care Is Not the Same for Men and Women

The quality of health care VA provides to women Veteran's exceeds the care many would receive in other settings (including commercially managed care systems, Medicare and Medicaid). For example, VA's system of quality management and preventive patient care, supported by technology like our electronic health record and clinical reminders, ensures women are screened for unique health concerns like cervical cancer or breast cancer at higher rates than non-VA health care programs. On the other hand, VA is aware of existing disparities between male and female Veterans in our system. The Department is particularly concerned with performance measures related to cardiovascular disease, the leading cause of death in women. Performance scores for several quality measures, including high blood pressure, high cholesterol and diabetes, all of which contribute to cardiovascular disease risk, show a consistent difference between men and women Veterans. Gender-neutral prevention measures such as colon cancer screening, depression screening and immunizations show a disparity between men and women Veterans as well. For example, although VA significantly outperforms Medicare on colorectal cancer screening, only 75 percent of women Veterans are screened compared with 83 percent of male Veterans. These issues and other quality issues are being addressed.

Some women report that lack of newborn care and child care forces them to seek care elsewhere. VA recently supported section 309 of S. 252, which would authorize VA to furnish health care services up to 7 days after birth to a newborn child of a female Veteran who is receiving maternity care furnished by VA if the Veteran delivered the child in a VA health care facility or in another facility pursuant to a contract for service related to such delivery. We similarly supported a companion measure in the House. We believe benefits such as these will help improve women Veterans' perception that VA welcomes them and will provide complete, effective and compassionate care.

Current Initiatives Target Improved Care

VA recognizes the need to continually improve our services to women Veterans, and has initiated new programs including the implementation of comprehensive primary care throughout the nation, enhancing mental health for women Veterans, staffing every VA medical center with a women Veterans program manager, creating a mini-residency education program on women's health for primary care physicians, supporting a multi-faceted research program on women's health, improving communication and outreach to women Veterans, and continuing the operation of organizations like the Center for Women Veterans and the Women Veterans Health Strategic Healthcare Group.

Comprehensive Primary Care for Women Veterans

VA is implementing an innovative approach to women's health care that seeks to reduce the possibilities of fragmented care, quality disparities, and lack of provider proficiency in women's health by fundamentally changing the experience of women Veterans in VA.

In March 2008, the former Under Secretary for Health charged a workgroup to define necessary actions for ensuring every woman Veteran has access to a VA primary care provider capable of meeting all her primary care needs, including gender-specific and mental health care, in the context of a continuous patient-clinician relationship. This new definition places a strong emphasis on improved coordination of care for women Veterans, continuity, and patient-centeredness. In November 2008, the workgroup released its final report identifying recommendations for delivering comprehensive primary care. These recommendations included: (1) delivering coordinated, comprehensive primary women's health care at every VA health care facility by recognizing best practices and developing systems and structure for care delivery appropriate to women Veterans; (2) integrating women's mental health care as part of primary care, including co-locating mental health providers; (3) promoting and incentivizing innovation in care delivery by supporting local best practices; (4) cultivating and enhancing capabilities of all VA staff to meet the comprehensive health care needs of women Veterans; and (5) achieving gender equity in the provision of clinical care. . . .

Access and wait times are better at sites where gender-specific services are available in an integrated women's primary care setting.

To achieve the goal of providing comprehensive primary care for women Veterans, VA has designed three models to promote the delivery of optimal primary care. Under the first model, women Veterans are seen within a gender neutral primary care clinic. Under the second model, women Veterans are seen in a separate but shared space that may be located within or adjacent to a primary care clinic. Under the third model, women Veterans are seen in an exclusive separate space with a separate entrance into the clinical area and a distinct waiting room. In this scenario, gynecological, mental health and social work services are co-located in this space. Each of these models can be tailored to local needs and conditions to systemize the coordination, continuity, and integration of women Veterans' care. One-third of VA facilities have already adopted the third model of comprehensive primary care delivery and found it to be very effective. Access and wait times are better at sites where gender-specific services are available in an integrated women's primary care setting, regardless of whether the care was delivered in a separate space (such as a women's clinic) or incorporated within general primary care clinics. VA facilities that have established a "one-stop" approach to primary care delivery have already reported higher patient satisfaction on care coordination for contraception, sexually transmitted disease screening, and menopausal management.

In addition to improving the primary care infrastructure for women Veterans, VA is committed to advancing the entire range of emergency, acute, and chronic health care services needed by women Veterans to develop an optimal continuum of health care. Such a continuum of health care includes: enhancing and integrating mental health care, medical and surgical specialty care, health promotion and disease prevention, diagnostic services and rehabilitation for catastrophic injuries.

Enhancing Mental Health

VA has identified that 37 percent of women Veterans who use VA health care have a mental health diagnosis; these rates are higher than those of male Veterans. Women Veterans also present with complex mental health needs, including depression, post-traumatic stress disorder (PTSD), military sexual trauma (MST), and parenting and family issues.

In response, VA has instituted policy requirements, such as that outlined in its Handbook on Uniform Mental Health Services in VA Medical Centers and Clinics, to emphasize the importance of being aware of gender-specific issues when providing mental health care. In particular, the Handbook identifies services every health care facility must have available for women Veterans to ensure integrated mental health services as a part of comprehensive primary care for women Veterans. For example, the services provided optimally involve a designated, co-located, collaborative provider (psychologist, social worker, or psychiatrist) and care management with an emphasis on the need for safety, privacy, dignity, and respect to characterize all gender-specific services provided. Facilities are strongly encouraged to give patients treated for other mental health conditions the option of a consultation from a same-sex provider regarding gender-specific issues. All inpatient and residential care facilities must provide separate and secured sleeping accommodations for women. Every VA facility has a designated MST coordinator who serves as a contact person for related issues. VA is ensuring a concerted effort to provide quality mental health care appropriate to the needs of women Veterans.

As of June 2009, each of VA's 144 health care systems has appointed a full-time Women Veterans Program Manager.

Women Veterans Program Managers

In order to ensure improved advocacy for women Veterans at the facility level, VA has mandated all VA medical centers appoint a full-time Women Veterans Program Manager. These Women Veterans Program Managers support increased outreach to women Veterans, improve quality of care provision, and develop best practices in organizational delivery of women's health care. They serve as advisors to facility directors in identifying and expanding the availability and access of inpatient and outpatient services for women Veterans and provide counseling on a range of gender-specific care issues. Women Veterans Program Managers also coordinate and provide appropriate local outreach initiatives to women Veterans.

As of June 2009, each of VA's 144 health care systems has appointed a full-time Women Veterans Program Manager.

Mini-Residency Training in Women's Health

As the number of women Veterans continues to grow, particularly women of childbearing age, VA recognizes many primary care providers need to update their women-specific clinical experience. VA is offering waves of mini-residencies in women's health across the country in strategic geographic locations. Each mini-residency lasts two and a half days and is taught by national women's health experts. Clinical staff receive presentations on contraception, cervical cancer screening and sexually transmitted infections, abnormal uterine bleeding, chronic abdominal and pelvic pain, post-deployment readjustment issues for women Veterans, and other womens' health topics. Early results from this program indicate its success in increasing competencies in 12 areas of women's health care. As of June 2009, 216 participants (119 physicians, 77 nurse practitioners, 10 physician assistants, 9 registered nurses and 1 therapist) from 90 VA medical centers and 28 community-based outpatient clinics have either scheduled or completed this program.

Research on Women Veteran's Health Issues

VA has clearly established women's health as a research priority and intensified its efforts in the last decade. Currently, VA's Office of Research and Development supports a broad research portfolio focused on women's health issues, including studies on diseases prevalent solely or predominantly in women, hormonal effects on diseases in post-menopausal women, and health needs and health care of women Veterans. VA's Office of Health Services Research and Development is funding 27 research projects in this area. VA is also conducting a study that will survey 3,500 women Veterans (both those who use VA health care and those who do not) to identify the changing health care needs of women Veterans and to understand the barriers they face in using VA health care. We anticipate receiving the results of this study within the next several months, and we will share these findings with the Committee. VA is also conducting risk assessments to track the effects of deployments on women Veterans and improve our epidemiological data on Operation Enduring Freedom/Operation Iraqi Freedom (OEF/OIF) women Veterans through the National Health Study for a New Generation of U.S. Veterans (an OEF/OIF cohort study). We are enrolling 60,000 Veterans for this study—of these 12,000 are women.

Outreach Initiatives

Effective internal and external communication and outreach to women Veterans is critical to the success of implementing comprehensive care. Surveys and research show that women Veterans are often not aware of the services and benefits available to them. VA is engaging in multiple efforts to correct this. For example, VA's Center for Women Veterans and the Women Veterans Health Strategic Health Care Group will continue to expand its ongoing outreach and communications plan to ensure increased public awareness of women Veterans and their service to our country and increased awareness by women Veterans of VA health care.

Center for Women Veterans

The Center's mission is to ensure that women Veterans have access to VA benefits and services on par with male Veterans; that VA programs are responsive to the gender-specific needs of women Veterans; that joint outreach is performed to improve women Veterans' awareness of VA services, benefits, and eligibility criteria; and that women Veterans are treated with dignity and respect. The Center coordinates and collaborates with Federal, State and local agencies, Veterans service organizations and community-based organizations.

Women Veterans Health Strategic Healthcare Group

VA has developed a women Veterans health care "brand" within VA and among women Veterans. VA has made available upgraded communication resources, processes, and tools to

Veterans Integrated Service Networks (VISN) and facilities. VA is building on the OEF/OIF call center to reach out to women Veterans. New scripts, new outreach materials and training are being developed to ensure women Veterans are aware of VA's services and benefits. While these efforts have created an important foundation upon which to build, it will take sustained and coordinated planning to successfully reach out to women Veterans.

Future Plans

While significant efforts are underway, we recognize that more must be done. VA must provide recurring funds to build adequate infrastructure for primary care and expand services to provide a full continuum of care for women Veterans at its secondary and tertiary care facilities. This investment of resources will contribute to the continuing goal of delivering quality health care focused on privacy, safety, sensitivity, dignity and continuity.

11

Better Treatment Options Are Needed for Victims of Military Sexual Trauma

U.S. Medicine: The Voice of Federal Medicine

U.S. Medicine is a monthly publication that serves healthcare professionals working in the Department of Veterans Affairs, Department of Defense, and US Public Health Service.

Victims of military sexual trauma (MST) struggle with the same physical, emotional and psychological issues as civilians who are victims of sexual abuse, but the lingering effects can be more intense because of the likelihood that the perpetrators are their peers, and in some cases, their supervisors. While the Department of Veterans Affairs routinely screens veterans for MST, critics have complained that the availability of services for victims is limited, and that what services are available are often poorly planned and poorly publicized. More research is needed to understand the impact of MST on women veterans.

For a civilian victim of sexual assault, the after-effects are devastating. There's the physical, emotional, and psychological trauma to contend with, as well as having to navigate a world that seems more dangerous than it did before.

For a military servicemember dealing with sexual trauma, these after-effects are compounded by the fact that the perpetrators are almost always their peers—the people they live with and work with—and are sometimes their supervisors. For a victim of military sexual trauma (MST), it can be seemingly impossible to find a place to feel safe, and even seeking treatment can unintentionally force them to relive the initial trauma.

MST Puts Careers at Risk

"Perpetrators are frequently peers or supervisors responsible for the decisions on work-related evaluations and promotions," explained Rep John Hall, D-NY, chair of the VA [Department of Veterans Affairs] subcommittee on disability assistance, at a hearing on benefits and treatment options for MST last month. "This means that victims must choose between continuing their military careers at the expense of frequent contact with their perpetrators, or ending their careers in order to protect themselves. Many victims share that when they do report the incident, they are not believed or are encouraged to keep silent because of the need to preserve organizational cohesion.

"There also has been frustration with the lack of appropriate healthcare providers to treat veterans who have experience working with MST. VA and DoD [Department of Defense] need to ensure that proper treatment is available."

Both VA and DoD have made significant progress in recent years in training healthcare providers in recognizing and treating the effects of MST. However, as legislators learned last month, there is still a long way to go before victims of MST can get proper care in a nonthreatening environment.

VA Screening, Treatment

"It is important to remember that MST is an experience, not a diagnosis or a mental health condition in and of itself," declared Susan McCutcheon, RN, EdD, VA's director of military sexual trauma, at last month's hearing. "There is no one way that everyone will respond. For some veterans, MST will continue to affect their mental and physical health many years later. Fortunately, people can recover, and VA has services to do that."

Since 1992, VA has been developing programs to monitor MST screening and treatment, providing staff with training on most MST issues. Most recently, VA established a national-level MST Support Team to help further all MST-related objectives.

All veterans seeking care at VA are asked two questions: one to assess sexual harassment, and one to assess sexual assault. "Any that answer yes to either question are asked if they are interested in treatment," McCutcheon said. "VA data indicates that approximately 1 in 5 women and 1 in 100 men seen at VA respond yes when asked about MST."

McCutcheon noted that, because of the high proportion of men to women in the military, there are actually only slightly fewer men than women seen in VA who have experienced MST.

Every VA facility has a designated MST coordinator who serves as a contact point for patients, helping them find and access VA services. Many facilities have outpatient mental health services focusing on sexual trauma, and some have inpatient programs. There are also single-gender programs to accommodate veterans who do not feel comfortable in mixed-gender treatment.

VA Programs—Few and Hidden

While these initiatives by VA show the agency has the right idea, they are few and far between, veterans' advocates say. According to GAO [Government Accountability Office], only 9 of 153 medical centers nationally have residential treatment programs for women suffering from mental health injuries. When GAO investigators began researching VA programs, they had trouble discovering which VA facilities had what programs.

"VA's website did not provide a complete list of facilities that provided MST programs," according to Jennifer Hunt, project coordinator for the Iraq and Afghanistan Veterans of America (IAVA).

One of IAVA's top recommendations is for VA to do a better job of advertising its MST programs. "According to one IAVA member, she did not know until three years after returning from a deployment that VA provided sexual trauma counseling," Hunt said. "In her words, 'It's well-hidden and not talked about at VA.'"

VA medical centers ought to have separate facilities for women patients, and easy, safe, and direct access to MST treatment areas for both male and female MST survivors.

More Inpatient Treatment Options Are Needed

Another concern is that inpatient mental health services and gender-specific programs are just too sparse. "VA must expand availability of its specialized sexual trauma treatment in the inpatient setting. Less than 10% of VA medical centers offer inpatient treatment for MST. IAVA recommends that every VISN [Veterans Integrated Service Network] offer at least one inpatient setting specializing in care for MST victims," Hunt said. "And victims should not have to settle for mixed-gender options because there are no [VA] treatment programs in their area."

Mixed-gender treatment programs can be an unacceptable solution for an MST patient, who does not want to discuss or relive the trauma among members of the opposite gender.

"VA medical centers ought to have separate facilities for women patients, and easy, safe, and direct access to MST treatment areas for both male and female MST survivors," said Anuradha Bhagwati, executive director of the Service Women's Action Network (SWAN). "Another disturbing trend is VA's integration of residential programs with other mixed-gender veterans' programs, in which MST patients are not guaranteed privacy or safety from other patients of the opposite sex. VA needs to invest in separate facilities for MST programs, and guarantee the safety and welfare of all participants."

Sexual assault can be a common trigger for post-traumatic stress disorder, which researchers ... are finding presents differently in women than in men.

Gender-Specific Research

Not enough is known about the physical and mental health consequences of MST, or how those consequences differ between men and women. According to Phyllis Greenberger, president of the Society for Women's Health Research, studies in the area of MST and sexual assault have revealed interesting sex-based differences that need to be explored further to help improve treatment methods.

"First, women are more likely than men to contract a sexually transmitted infection, or STI. STIs are often more difficult to treat in women and can have emotional and mental impacts over a woman's lifespan," Greenberger noted. "The impacts of MST are not limited to reproduction. Infection with HPV after a sexual assault can result in cancer decades later."

Also, sexual assault can be a common trigger for post-traumatic stress disorder, which researchers—many of whom are based in VA facilities—are finding presents differently in women than in men. "Women do not respond the same to some of the common medications prescribed for PTSD, often faring worse than men taking the same medication for the same diagnosis," Greenberger explained. "[Also] multiple traumas can increase the likelihood of developing PTSD, and the combined impacts of working in a war zone, multiple deployments, MST, and for a disproportionate share of female military members, exposure to early life trauma, all raise the risk for an eventual PTSD diagnosis. Females in the military have twice the levels of PTSD and depression as their male counterparts."

Women Are at Greater Risk

Research also suggests that the ultimate impact of a traumatic event on a woman may depend on hormone levels. "The role of cyclical hormonal variations, as well as studies finding that during pregnancy PTSD symptoms decrease, may offer insight into which women develop PTSD after MST, and may further help discover more effective PTSD therapies for women—therapies that are responsive to sex-based hormonal differences," Greenberger explained. "There is clearly a need for more sex-based research at VA."

At the very least, a better understanding by VA physicians of MST and its effects could help veterans suffering from it to feel more comfortable seeking VA treatment. "Many veterans are ignored, isolated, or misunderstood at VA facilities because their PTSD is not combat-related. The veterans' community still primarily considers PTSD to be a combat-related condition, to the great detriment of MST survivors," Bhagwati noted. "Survivors who have used the VA routinely say they are fed up with being given endless prescription medication—one Iraq veteran described the experience of her VA MST treatment as nothing but 'pills and pep talks.'"

She recommended that VA allow MST survivors to seek fee-based care where they feel most comfortable, if such care is not provided by their local VA facility, including giving them access to alternative treatments, such as yoga, massage therapy, and acupuncture.

12

Veterans' Health Care Has Improved, but Racial Disparities Exist

David Orenstein

David Orenstein is a writer in the Department of News and Communication at Brown University.

Two recent studies show significant improvement in the quality of health care provided at 142 Veterans Administration health facilities. At the same time, the studies show that significant differences continue to persist in the quality of care received by black and white veterans.

As recently as the 1990s, the Veterans Affairs health care system had a subpar reputation for quality, but two new studies of standard quality metrics, both led by Amal Trivedi, assistant professor of community health at Brown University and a physician at the Providence VA Medical Center, show that the system that cares for more than 5 million patients has improved markedly in the last decade.

In one study, published March 18 [2011] in the journal *Medical Care*, Trivedi found that the VA's care for seniors is consistently better than what is available through private Medicare Advantage plans, but another analysis published in the April issue of *Health Affairs* shows that while care has improved for both black and white patients, racial disparities persist in health outcomes.

Trivedi, who receives some of his funding from the VA, said each peer-reviewed analysis was based on widely accepted processes given the patient's condition and whether patients experienced favorable outcomes. For example, for patients with diabetes, quality care requires both testing and controlling their cholesterol. In his studies, Trivedi and his co-authors analyzed millions of documented cases of care delivery.

In 2009, 63 percent of black veterans with diabetes had controlled cholesterol compared to 71 percent of white veterans, a disparity of 8 percentage points. In 2005, the disparity was 9 percentage points.

The Race Gap

For the analysis published in *Health Affairs*, Trivedi studied 10 quality indicators in the records of more than 1.1 million veterans. He found that during the last decade, VA doctors became significantly more likely to provide better care to members of each racial group, both for process (ordering appropriate tests) and outcomes (obtaining improved results). But because care for black veterans did not increase in quality faster than it did for white veterans, the disparity that existed before has remained stubbornly in place.

"The disparities that we saw were for outcomes measures, or getting the right result, as opposed to the provider doing the correct thing," said Trivedi, who teaches in Brown's Department of Community Health and sees patients as a hospitalist at the Providence VA Medical Center.

For example, in 2009, 63 percent of black veterans with diabetes had controlled cholesterol compared to 71 percent of white veterans, a disparity of 8 percentage points. In 2005, the disparity was 9 percentage points.

While the disparity didn't change, the quality of care did. Among patients with diabetes, only 52 percent of black veterans and only 61 percent of white veterans had controlled cholesterol in 2005. Between 2005 and 2009, whites and blacks saw 10 and 11 percentage-point jumps in better outcomes respectively.

Disparities Are Common

Trivedi and co-authors Regina Crebla, Steven Wright, and Donna Washington said that the disparity is not found in just a few VA medical centers, but persists widely throughout the system.

He said the study can't account for why the gap has remained even though the VA has improved quality overall, but the data present the VA with the opportunity to recognize the disparity and focus on it.

"I think it's important for all health systems, not just the VA, to track performance for vulnerable groups," he said.

Other research, he said, has shown that racial disparities on similar measures is 1.3 to 2 times higher in the Medicare system than at the VA.

Advantage for Seniors

Overall, the VA trumps private Medicare plans for patients 65 and older, according to the analysis Trivedi published in *Medical Care* last month. With co-author Crebla, Trivedi looked at comparable quality indicators in 293,000 VA records from 142 VA medical centers and more than 5.7 million from 305 Medicare Advantage plans between 2000 and 2007.

"On these indicators the VA outperformed private sector Medicare Advantage plans by a wide and increasing margin," Trivedi said. "Quality is going to be a function of incentives and capabilities, and in the VA the incentives may be better aligned for providing high-quality care."

In the study's first year, Trivedi said, the VA system scored higher in 10 of 11 quality measures, missing the mark only on providing eye exams to diabetic patients, by 2.6 percentage points.

After the first year, the VA's quality improved faster than the private plans in a majority of indicators. By the final year in the study, Trivedi said, the VA surpassed Medicare Advantage providers in all 12 measures he studied.

The VA's higher quality margin in 2007 ranged from 4.3 percentage points in the case of testing LDL cholesterol among patients with coronary artery disease to 30.8 percentage points in providing colorectal cancer screening.

In all 12 measures, the VA also had lower quality disparities than private plans between patients living in areas with the highest and lowest incomes and education levels. For example, for diabetic patients, the quality difference in controlling blood sugar between patients living in the richest and poorest areas was 0.6 percentage points in the VA system, compared to 8.1 percentage points in Medicare Advantage plans.

"The VA holds clinicians and managers accountable for quality, and emphasizes primary care and health information technology," Trivedi said. "These practices can also be used by private-sector systems to improve care."

In addition to the VA, the Robert Wood Johnson Foundation funded the studies published in *Medical Care* and *Health Affairs*.

Organizations to Contact

The editors have compiled the following list of organizations concerned with the issues debated in this book. The descriptions are derived from materials provided by the organizations. All have publications or information available for interested readers. The list was compiled on the date of publication of the present volume; names; addresses, phone and fax numbers, and e-mail and Internet addresses may change. Be aware that many organizations take several weeks or longer to respond to inquiries, so allow as much time as possible.

The American Legion
700 N. Pennsylvania St., Indianapolis, IN   46206
(317) 630-1200 • fax: (317) 630-1223
website: www.legion.org

The American Legion, chartered by Congress in 1919, is the largest veterans' service organization in the United States. Comprehensive information about American Legion services to veterans, including assistance calculating benefits, enrolling for VA benefits, and seeking help with PTSD, is available on the organization's website. The website also provides information on legislative priorities and advocacy.

National Institute of Neurological Disorders and Stroke
PO Box 5801, Bethesda, MD   20824
(800) 352-9424
website: www.ninds.nih.gov

The National Institute of Neurological Disorders and Stroke (NINDS), part of the National Institutes of Health, conducts research on the causes, prevention, diagnosis and treatment of neurological disorders, including traumatic brain injury, a disorder that affects many veterans of Iraq and Afghanistan. The NINDS website includes detailed information about traumatic brain injury research and ongoing clinical trials.

National Veterans Foundation
9841 Airport Blvd., Suite 418, Los Angeles, CA   90045
(310) 642-0255 • fax: (310) 642-0258
website: www.nvf.org

The National Veterans Foundation is a veteran-run non-profit human service organization committed to serving the crisis and information needs of veterans and their families. Services provided include emotional support, referrals for medical treatment, substance abuse and PTSD counseling, VA benefits advocacy, food, shelter, employment training, legal aid, and suicide intervention. The Department of Veterans Affairs Benefits Booklet, which provides detailed information about accessing services for veterans, is posted on the NVF website. The website also includes a list of Departments of Veterans Affairs locations.

National Veterans Legal Services Program
PO Box 65762, Washington, DC   20035
(202) 265-8305 • fax: (202) 328-0063
e-mail: info@nvlsp.org
website: www.nvlsp.org

The National Veterans Legal Services Program is a nonprofit organization that recruits, trains, and assists lawyer and non-lawyer advocates who represent veterans and active duty military personnel free of charge. According to the organization's website, lawsuits brought by NVLSP attorneys have resulted in the Department of Veterans Affairs (VA) paying hundreds of millions of dollars in benefits to disabled veterans and their families, and in military departments returning millions of dollars in back pay to veterans.

Paralyzed Veterans of America
801 Eighteenth Street NW, Washington, DC   20006-3517
(800) 424-8200
e-mail: info@pva.org
website: www.pva.org

Paralyzed Veterans of America was founded by a group of veterans who returned from their service in WWII with spinal cord injuries. The organization strives to create brighter futures and improved quality of life for veterans by supporting medical research in areas related to spinal cord injuries and rehabilitation. It advocates for the health care rights and other rights of injured service members.

US Department of Veterans Affairs Veterans Health Administration

810 Vermont Avenue NW, Washington, DC   20420
website: www.va.gov

The Veterans Health Administration is an integrated health care system that serves more than 8.3 million veterans each year. The Veterans Health Administration website provides contact information for 23 Veterans Integrated Services Networks located throughout the United States. A benefits booklet, *Federal Benefits for Veterans, Dependents, and Survivors,* is also posted on the Veterans Health Administration website.

US National Library of Medicine

8600 Rockville Pike, Bethesda, MD   20894
(301) 594-5983 • fax: (301) 402-1384
website: www.nlm.nih.gov

The US National Library of Medicine (NLM) is the world's largest medical library. The library collects materials and provides information and research services in all areas of biomedicine and health care. The Medline Plus website, produced by NLM, contains consumer health information about diseases, conditions, and wellness issues, written in clear and easily understood language. MedlinePlus contains extensive information about health issues faced by veterans, which can be accessed by searching with the keyword "veterans."

Veterans Crisis Line

(800) 273-8255 ext. 1
website: www.veteranscrisisline.net

The Veterans Crisis Line, staffed by the Department of Veterans Affairs, provides crisis counseling and support to veterans and their families and friends. The Veterans Crisis Line can be reached through a confidential toll-free hotline, online chat, or text. The website includes extensive information on resources available to address the mental health needs of veterans and those who are close to them.

Veterans Health Council

(301) 585-4000

e-mail: vhc@veteranshealth.org

website: www.veteranshealth.org

The mission of the Veterans Health Council is to create a forum for exchange of information about specific health care concerns as well as services available for veterans of the Vietnam War, the Persian Gulf War and the Global War on Terror.

Veterans of Modern Warfare

PO Box 96503, Washington, DC   20090-6503

(888) 445-9891

website: www.vmwusa.org

Veterans of Modern Warfare (VMW) is a veterans service organization that focuses on the needs of veterans who have served in the military since 1990. VMW provides education and information about benefits available to veteran and offers assistance in obtaining benefits. The organization engages in advocacy about issues important to veterans who served during the last 20 years.

Wounded Warriors Project

4899 Belfort Road, Suite 300, Jacksonville, FL   32256

(904) 296-7350 • fax: (904) 296-7347

website: www.woundedwarriorproject.org/

The mission of the Wounded Warriors Project is to raise the public's awareness and enlist its aid in support of the needs of injured service members, to mobilize injured service members to provide aid and assistance to one another, and to develop programs to meet the needs of injured service members.

Bibliography

Books

Penny Coleman   *Flashback: Posttraumatic Stress Disorder, Suicide, and the Lessons of War.* Boston: Beacon Press, 2006.

Patricia P. Driscoll *Hidden Battles on Unseen Fronts:*
and Celia Straus   *Stories of American Soldiers with Traumatic Brain Injury and PTSD.* Drexel Hill, PA: Casemate, 2009.

Erin P. Finley   *Fields of Combat: Understanding PTSD Among Veterans of Iraq and Afghanistan.* Ithaca, NY: Cornell University Press, 2011.

David A. Gerber,   *Disabled Veterans in History.* Ann
ed.   Arbor: University of Michigan Press, 2000.

Aaron Glantz   *The War Comes Home: Washington's Battle Against America's Veterans.* Berkeley: University of California Press, 2009.

Heidi L.W.   *Potential Costs of Veterans' Health*
Golding   *Care,* Congress of the United States, Government Printing Office, 2010.

Janelle Hill,   *Life After the Military: A Handbook*
Cheryl Lawhorne,   *for Transitioning Veterans.* Lanham,
and Don Philpott   MD: Government Institutes, 2011.

Margaret C.   *Veterans' Rights and Benefits.* New
Jasper   York: Oceana, 2009.

James D. Johnson · *Combat Trauma: A Personal Look at Long-Term Consequences.* Lanham, MD: Rowman & Littlefield Publishers, 2010.

Martin Kantor · *Uncle Sam's Shame: Inside Our Broken Veterans Administration.* Westport, CT: Praeger Security International, 2008.

Lawrence J. Korb · *Serving America's Veterans: A Reference Handbook.* Santa Barbara, CA: Praeger Security International, 2009.

Yvonne Latty · *In Conflict: Iraq War Veterans Speak Out on Duty, Loss and the Fight to Stay Alive.* Sausalito, CA: PoliPoint Press, 2006.

Suzanne Mettler · *Soldiers to Citizens: The G.I. Bill and the Making of the Greatest Generation.* New York: Oxford University Press, 2005.

Richard F. Mollica · *Healing Invisible Wounds: Paths to Hope and Recovery in a Violent World.* Orlando, FL: Harcourt, 2006.

Victor Montgomery III · *Healing Suicidal Veterans: Recognizing, Supporting and Answering Their Pleas for Help.* Far Hills, NJ: New Horizon Press, 2009.

James W. Parkinson and Lee Benson · *Soldier Slaves: Abandoned by White House, Courts, and Congress.* Annapolis, MD: Naval Institute Press, 2006.

Martin Schram	*Vets Under Siege: How America Deceives and Dishonors Those Who Fight Our Battles.* New York: Thomas Dunne Books, 2008.
Jonathan Shay	*Odysseus in America: Combat Trauma and the Trials of Homecoming.* New York: Scribner, 2002.
Richard Taylor and Sandra Wright Taylor	*Homeward Bound: American Veterans Return From War.* Westport, Conn: Praeger Security International, 2007.

Periodicals and Internet Sources

Lizette Alvarez	"War Veterans' Concussions are Often Overlooked," *New York Times,* August 26, 2008.
Business Wire	"Veterans Praise President's Support for Health Care Funding Reform," April 9, 2009.
James Dao	"Pentagon Plans to Consolidate Military Health Records," *New York Times,* May 26, 2011.
James Dao	"Veterans Affairs Faces Surge of Disability Claims," *New York Times,* July 13, 2009.
Faye Fiore	"Female Veteran Fights an Invisible Injury," *Los Angeles Times,* April 9, 2011.
Laura Fitzpatrick	"Landmark Bill Bolsters Care for Female Veterans," *TIME,* May 5, 2010.

Dahleen Glanton   "Iraq War is Over, But Effects Linger
                         for Veterans," *Chicago Tribune*,
                         December 20, 2011.

Steve Griffin   "Combat Injuries Can Change Lives
                         in Surprising Ways," *New York Times*,
                         November 14, 2011.

iHealthBeat   "VA Announces Launch of Facebook
                         Pages for all 152 Medical Centers,"
                         December 22, 2011.

Lee Hill   "Veteran Benefits Inflate Rising Cost
Kavanaugh and   of War: Analysis of Disability Rolls
Chris Adams   Finds Today's Veterans are More
                         Likely to Seek Benefits," *Kansas City
                         Star*, December 16, 2011.

Sarah Kiff   "Defense Has a Health Care
                         Spending Problem," *Washington Post*,
                         January 6, 2012.

Jami Kinton   "Injured Veteran Not Giving Up,"
                         Mansfield News Journal, December
                         12, 2011.

Paul R.   "Retired Chaplain Says Veterans of
Kopenkoskey   Iraq War May Grapple with 'Moral
                         Injury'," *Grand Rapids Press*,
                         December 17, 2011.

Julia Love   "Answers About VA's New
                         Stress-Disorder Policy," *Los Angeles
                         Times*, July 13, 2010.

Kim Murphy   "Did the War Make Him Do It?" *Los
                         Angeles Times*, November 28, 2009.

New York Times	"The V.A. Tries to Get Beyond Its Culture of No," July 16, 2011.
New York Times	"More Excuses and Delays from the V.A.," August 21, 2011.
New York Times	"Help for Homeless Veterans," December 18, 2011.
Nate Rawlings	"The Real Medical Legacy of America's Wars," *TIME*, 2011.
Peter Spiegel	"Psych Exams Urged for Vets," *Los Angeles Times*, September 21, 2008.
Mark Thompson	"Purple Hearts for Psychic Scars?" *TIME*, June 8, 2008.
Mark Thompson	"The $1 Trillion Bill for Bush's War on Terror," *TIME*, December 26, 2008.
Michael Weisskopf	"Veterans Day in Court," *TIME*, January 12, 2008.
Ron Wyden	"Is the Administration Leaving a Promising Health Reform in the Cold?" *Huffington Post*, December 12, 2011.
Greg Zoroya	"360,000 Veterans May Have Brain Injuries," *USA Today*, March 5, 2009.
David Zucchino	"For Parents, Their Own Trauma," *Los Angeles Times*, December 14, 2008.

Index

A

Abe, Gary, 48–49
Active duty personnel health care
    cost increases, 14, 42
    increasing suicide levels, 9, 61
    overview, 10–18
    transition to veteran status,
      15, 17, 35–36
Afghanistan War (2001–)
    epidemiological research on
      veterans, 76
    guarantee of care after de-
      ployment, 29
    mental health conditions in
      returning troops, 16, 37–38,
      50, 59, 61
    projected costs increasing,
      40–41, 42–44
    rural veterans, 50, 52
    stresses VA medical system,
      49–50
    women veterans increasing in
      number, 69
Agent Orange exposure, 28
Ahrens, James F., 55
Altman, Jake, 34
Associated Press, 47–51

B

Bair, Byron, 54
Bhagwati, Anuradha, 82
Bilmes, Linda, 41, 42, 43–44, 45
Budget for military and veterans'
    health care. *See* Funding of mili-
    tary and veterans' health care

C

Cagle, Bob, 60, 63, 65, 66–67
Cancer screening, 70–71
Cardiovascular disease, gender
    disparities, 70
Center for Women Veterans, 76
Chard, Kate, 29, 30–31
Cholesterol control, racial dispari-
    ties, 85–86
Civilian Health and Medical Pro-
    gram of the Department of Vet-
    erans Affairs (CHAMPVA), 14
Claims backlog cases, 7–8, 50,
    56–59
Clinics and medical centers
      primary care, 72–73
      rural community-based, 50,
        53, 54, 59
      Veterans Centers, 31
      women veterans, 23–24, 69–
        70, 72–73, 80–81
      Women Veterans Program
        Managers, 74–75
Conti, Samuel, 58
Corteville, Shelley, 60, 64, 65–66
Court cases, claims backlogs, 7–8,
    50, 56–59
Crebla, Regina, 86

D

Dahlstedt, Kate, 65
Department of Defense. *See* US
    Department of Defense (DoD)

PTSD. *See* Post-traumatic stress
disorder (PTSD)

Q

Quality of health care
    initiatives by VA and DoD, 15
    needs of women veterans,
      68–77
    racial disparities exist, 84–87
    VA care is among best in the
      US, 19–24
    VA care is inadequate, 25–32

R

Racial disparities in health care,
  84–87
Rape. *See* Sexual trauma
Reinhardt, Stephen, 8, 57
Research
    moral injuries, 62–63, 64, 65
    racial disparities in care,
      84–87
    women veterans' health issues,
      75–76, 82–83
Retreats, as therapy for moral in-
  juries, 67
Rivera, Gil, 25–26, 27–28, 31–32
Rural veterans
    government aims to improve
      health care access, 52–55
    health care is not readily
      available, 47–51
    lack of suicide prevention of-
      ficers, 59

S

Schmidt, Ulrike, 62
Senior veterans, quality of care, 84

Servicemen's Readjustment Act
  (GI Bill; 1944), 38–39
Sexual trauma
    better treatment options are
      needed, 78–83
    Corteville (Shelley) case, 64,
      66
Sexually transmitted infections
  (STIs), 82
Share the Sacrifice Act, 46
Shay, Jonathan, 61, 62, 63
Sherman, Nancy, 62–63
Shinseki, Eric, 35, 37, 39
Silver, Diane, 60–67
Skupien, Mary Beth, 52
Social Security disability for veter-
  ans, 42
Soldier's Heart (organization),
  65–66
Spiritual and moral injuries,
  60–67
Stiglitz, Joseph, 41, 42, 43–44, 45
STIs (sexually transmitted
  infections), 82
Suicide
    greater numbers than combat
      deaths, 61
    increasing among veterans
      and service members, 9, 50,
      56–57
    lack of suicide prevention of-
      ficers, 59
    Vietnam War veterans, 63
Sullivan, Paul, 42, 45
Suran, Melissa, 25–32

T

Talk therapy, for moral injuries,
  64
Taylor, Josh, 49